S0-ADA-210

RENAISSANCE WOMEN IN SCIENCE

LOUISE Q. VAN DER DOES

RITA J. SIMON

University Press of America, Inc.
Lanham • New York • Oxford

Copyright © 2000 by
University Press of America,® Inc.
4720 Boston Way
Lanham, Maryland 20706

12 Hid's Copse Rd.
Cumnor Hill, Oxford OX2 9JJ

All rights reserved
Printed in the United States of America
British Library Cataloging in Publication Information Available

Library of Congress Cataloging-in-Publication Data

Van der Does, Louise Q.
Renaissance women in science / Louise Q. van der Does, Rita J. Simon.
p.   cm.
Includes index.
1. Women scientists—Biography. I. Simon, Rita J.   II. Title.
Q141.V25   1994   500'.82'0922—dc21   99—038106 CIP

ISBN 0-7618-1480-9 (cloth: alk. ppr.)
ISBN 0-7618-1481-7 (pbk: alk. ppr.)

⊖™ The paper used in this publication meets the minimum
requirements of American National Standard for Information
Sciences—Permanence of Paper for Printed Library Materials,
ANSI Z39.48—1984

Contents

Introduction

ℰⓇ

With this volume, we begin a series that celebrates women who have not only made momentous contributions in their disciplines, but whose personal lives and experiences make them worthy of the title "Renaissance Woman." When the word renaissance is mentioned, it calls to mind a period of rebirth, reawakening, and revival. The period known as the Renaissance was a time when the creative world emerged from the shelter of the Dark Ages and celebrated art and architecture, literature, and learning. During the nineteenth century, another renaissance took place — that of women in science. Women, traditionally relegated to domestic and family endeavors, began their own rebirth by pursuing interests traditionally dominated by men.

Contained in this book are the stories of sixteen female scientists who unlocked the secrets of the universe and helped change the future of the world. These women studied vastly different scientific disciplines, ranging from the cosmic reaches of astronomy to the infinitesimal mechanics of the atom. They are the daughters of many countries with varied political and religious backgrounds. They came from different social classes, some from small towns and humble beginnings, and others from wealthy and privileged families where intellectual pursuits were part of daily life. But no matter their background, all of these women shared a passion for and a dedication to their work — the work of scientific discovery.

One of the first of these women, Maria Mitchell, was an American astronomer, who was recognized for her work studying sunspots on the surfaces of both Jupiter and Saturn. Perhaps one of her most important contributions was her strong advocacy for the higher education of women. By championing the idea of schooling as a priority for women, she helped pave the way for generations of women, allowing them to fulfill their dreams in science and other traditionally male-dominated fields.

One woman who benefited from Mitchell's advocacy was Ellen H. S. Richards. Born a quarter of a century after Mitchell, she became one of the first women in America to be awarded a degree in science. Richards founded the American Home Economics Association, where she played a key role in improving domestic sanitary conditions by applying her knowledge of chemistry to household chores. Not only did she encourage other women to seek degrees, the application of her theories made the domestic life of women easier.

Making discoveries that would be helpful to others was not particular to Ellen Richards. Another American woman, Alice Hamilton, became a pioneer in the science of industrial technology. Hamilton was the preeminent authority on the various illnesses caused by poisons in the workplace. This was an enormous concern during the Industrial Revolution, especially because children comprised a large part of the workforce. Her humanitarian efforts included establishing an occupational disease commission in Illinois in 1910. The evolution of her advocacy can be witnessed today with the EPA, OSHA, and numerous other government agencies that work to protect the environment, both industrial and natural.

Hamilton's contemporary, Florence Rena Sabin, also used her knowledge to protect the welfare of others. The first female full professor at the Johns Hopkins Medical School, Sabin focused on researching blood vessels and tuberculosis, a very common disease of the time. She too bequeathed a humanitarian legacy. Through her tremendous efforts, eight health bills became law in 1947, ensuring that better health care would be a right and not a privilege.

While these women were able to pursue advanced degrees and make their way in the scientific world independently, many other women made their name in partnership with their scientist husbands. The most notable example of this is Marie Curie. A hardworking student since childhood, Marie continued her schooling after high school by joining a group of privately instructed students, as women were not admitted to the University of Warsaw. Later, she left her native Poland for Paris and enrolled at the

Sorbonne. It was in Paris that she met her husband, Pierre, and began the research that remains her best known today. Marie toiled in the lab along with Pierre and scientist Henri Becquerel. Pursuing fundamental research on radioactivity led the three to share a Nobel Prize in 1903 and, later, after her husband's death, Marie went on to claim a solo Nobel Prize in 1911 for her discovery and research of radium and polonium.

Another scientist who shared the laboratory with her husband was Lillian Moller Gilbreth, an American engineer. She and her husband, Frank Gilbreth, developed the "Time and Motion Study" to increase the efficiency and output of industry. Apparently applying this study to their own lives, the couple produced twelve children! Not surprisingly, Gilbreth was a pioneer of an industrial psychology that went beyond the mechanics of industry to consider the human element as well.

Gerty Theresa Radnitz Cori, a Czech-born American biochemist, teamed up with her husband, Carl Ferdinand Cori, and colleague, Bernardo A. Houssay, to win a Nobel Prize in 1947. Together, they discovered the intermediate steps in glycogen-glucose conversion. Gerty Cori's discoveries helped reveal how enzyme deficiencies can lead to congenital metabolic diseases, setting the groundwork for medical research to move toward treatment.

The achievements of these women in the early twentieth century paved the way for the next wave of women scientists — the nuclear and atomic researchers. Lise Meitner, an Austrian-Swedish physicist and mathematician, discovered the protactinum-231 isotope and investigated the disintegration products of radium, thorium, and actinium and the behavior of beta rays. Meitner also made a significant contribution to the development of the atomic bomb with her conclusions regarding nuclear fission.

A German-born American physicist, Maria Geoppert-Mayer, made her way in the scientific world due in part to her partnership with her husband, Joseph Mayer. After coming to America and finding limited success in the academic realm because of her gender, Geoppert-Mayer participated in many key projects, including the atomic bomb project, with the help of her husband and a few scientists who admired her knowledge — among them Enrico Fermi. She went on to win the 1963 Nobel Prize for physics with Eugene Wigner and Hans Jensen for their work in demonstrating the structure of protons and neutrons in an atomic nucleus.

The dedication of these women to their work was so strong that, although the devastating effects of war were all around them, they nevertheless stayed focused on their research. One scientist, Emmy Noether, was a German mathematician who made major contributions to the development of abstract algebra, studying the formal properties of algebraic operations. She earned an appointment at Gottingen University in 1919 and developed the theories of ideals and of non-commutative algebra. In 1933, the Nazis dismissed Noether and the other Jewish professors. She subsequently left Germany and came to the U.S. where she worked at both Bryn Mawr College and at the Institute for Advanced Study at Princeton University.

Rita Levi-Montalcini, an Italian-American developmental biologist, stayed in her native Italy during World War II despite the fact that Mussolini had allied with Hitler and she was forced underground because of her Jewish heritage. A strong-willed woman, Levi-Montalcini continued her work in makeshift labs in her home and managed to avoid being caught by the Nazis. Not long after the war was over, she came to the United States to pursue nerve tissue research in St. Louis. Working tirelessly, she ultimately proved her discovery of "nerve growth factor" and, in 1986, she received a Nobel Prize, along with Stanley Cohen, for their work.

Many extraordinary women of science were committed to mental and physical health issues. Leta Hollingworth, for example, was an educational psychologist who measured gender differences in various traits to demonstrate scientifically that women could function as well as men in both educational and professional endeavors. Years after Maria Mitchell began her advocacy for women's educational rights, Hollingworth followed with demonstrable proof that created further opportunities for women and placed them on more equal footing in society. Her work was groundbreaking at a time when psychology as a science was just beginning to be acknowledged and to influence the cultural life of America.

Living in a time when disease was often viewed as a mysterious force that had the power to wipe out entire communities, many women scientists worked to improve worldwide health. Tuberculosis, one of the world's most dreaded and often fatal diseases at that time, was widespread and the cure often involved as much faith as science. Florence Seibert was a biochemist whose work in purifying tuberculin had a tremendous impact on the treatment of this disease.

Dorothy Mary Crowfoot Hodgkin, an Egyptian-born British chemist, stressed the need for cures beyond developed nations, advocating for a scientific community committed to Third World countries. In 1964, Hodgkin won a Nobel Prize for her work in determining the structure of compounds needed to combat pernicious anemia. Her work in analyzing structures of other biochemicals has also laid a strong foundation for further research.

With today's scientific world pondering the moral and medical complexities of cloning techniques and the potential benefits of genetically altered food sources, it's easy to take for granted the stepping stones that led to uncovering the mysteries of DNA. Rosalind Franklin, a British biophysicist, used X-ray diffraction to reveal important facts concerning the structure of DNA. She discovered that phosphate groups lie on the outside of the molecule, and that the DNA chain is a helical structure.

Barbara McClintock was an American geneticist whose tireless work was also crucial to understanding key characteristics of genetic material and her research was later acknowledged as a major contribution to DNA research. McClintock found that certain genetic material, called "transposable elements," could shift position on a chromosome from generation to generation. This altered the expression of a gene and provided a key to understanding cell differentiation. McClintock received a Nobel Prize in 1983.

Sixteen amazing women — what motivated them? What allowed them to break beyond the barriers of their time and their gender to pursue their dreams? In many instances, there was a mentor involved, often someone at school who took an interest in a remarkable child. Many of these women had strong relationships with their fathers, and were encouraged to "think like men," and to attack their interests with confidence. In a few cases, these women viewed their mothers' domesticated lives as demeaning, and vowed to pursue more intellectual goals. Some watched close relatives or friends die, claimed by an illness that had no cure. This motivated them to search for an answer and to put an end to suffering where they could. The desire of these women to make a difference in the world, to unselfishly make life better through their discoveries, was the element that allowed them to excel and to generously share their triumphs with the world.

An unfaltering focus on their work made it possible for these women to overcome the many obstacles before them — from world wars to gender wars. Although all of these women faced seemingly insurmountable odds, the most striking characteristic they share is that they all boldly and enthusiastically embarked on their journeys in life. And who better to educate us about the journeys in life than a scientist?

The scientist dedicates herself to learning and discovery. When one truly commits to this path, only great things lie ahead. When you read about these brave women and their extraordinary lives, we hope you too will be inspired to reach beyond the ordinary. We are all capable of discovery. It is not just in some of us, *it is in all of us.*

The groundwork laid by these women still provides a strong foundation not only for today's scientists, but for today's women as well. The path was navigated by the renaissance women of the past and it is a path that will continue to unfold before us, with each generation clearing the way for the next. Later, when authors are moved to collect and publish biographies about another set of renaissance women in science, it will be interesting to compare the obstacles the women in the twenty-first century had to overcome before they achieved similar success. Will the women who come along a century from now also confront and overcome obstacles to their success in the professional world? Will they have to combat a society that not only does not value them for their work, but also endangers their existence? And how many of the women in the twenty-first century will similarly combine an illustrious career with marriage and a family? While we wait for the answers to these questions, we hope you will find pleasure and inspiration in reading about the lives of these extraordinary women.

There are several people to whom we owe a debt of thanks. Nina Roscher, Chair of the Chemistry Department at American University, provided us guidance in selecting women scientists who fell under our definition of "renaissance." Immense credit is due Nancy Sweeney, Jeremiah Sullivan, and Liz Whyte for their research assistance and significant contributions to this project. We would also like to thank Lisa Banks and Sarah Hammond for their thoughtful reviews and extensive editorial comments.

Chapter 1

ℰℭ

Maria Mitchell

In 1831, in the small, prosperous, sea-faring community of Nantucket Island, Massachusetts, a twelve-year-old girl named Maria Mitchell assisted her father in observing the solar eclipse. Fascinated by this brief glimpse into the mysteries of the heavens, Maria would spend the rest of her life diligently studying the skies from her island home. Based on her work and discoveries, Mitchell would one day be hailed as one of the greatest astronomers of her generation. Like Urania, the female muse of Ancient Greek mythology who oversaw the science of astronomy, Maria would be recognized by scientists and curious onlookers as the famous "lady of astronomy" who proved to the world that women, especially nineteenth-century women, could do more, much more, than just embroider samplers or oversee the household help. She would become America's first professional female astronomer and would be celebrated throughout the world.

Maria Mitchell was born on Nantucket Island in 1818 to William and Lydia Mitchell. She was the third of ten children. Her parents were Quakers and had a slightly different outlook on the intellectual capacities of women than did the majority of the nineteenth-century American society. The common wisdom of the day held that too much intellectual education would damage a woman's health, that the weaker vessel would be fractured

Source: The Nantucket Maria Mitchell Association

or destroyed by too much thought. The Quakers did not share this belief, and Maria was encouraged from a young age to exercise the power of her mind. It was primarily because of this background that Maria would seek a path away from the home and hearth, and towards the complex, scientific life of an astronomer.

Maria began attending private elementary schools at the age of four. When she was nine, Maria's father, who made his living as a sometime-cooper and amateur astronomer, established a free, private school that Maria began to attend. Her father was an unconventional teacher who stressed field work in his educational curriculum. Students were taught about the natural world around them through direct observation and the collection of natural artifacts such as stones, flowers, and seashells. This hands-on, workman-like approach to scientific study had a profound effect on Maria who, throughout her life, believed persistence and hard work were the keys to success in all areas of life.

Around this time Maria began to help her father with his astronomy. It was part of the routine of raising the Mitchell children that their father taught them each as they grew all he knew about the stars and the spinning planets of our solar system and, as they became old enough, they would assist him in his own studies. Although not a serious scientist, Maria's father performed work on the rooftop of their house that was very important to the Nantucket community. The majority of the island population made its living off the sea. They were whalers and fisherman who had no recourse to the fancy electronic tracking devices that sailors today take for granted. Instead, they relied entirely on the stars and the compass for nautical navigation. William Mitchell was their guide post. Because of his daily observations, he had the most accurate and current astronomical records on the island. The whalers and fishermen would come to him to check the accuracy of their charts, sextants, and chronometers. Maria herself expressed the importance of this environment on her future:

> The spirit of the place had also much to do with the early bent of my mind in this direction [astronomy]. In Nantucket people quite generally are in the habit of observing the heavens, and a sextant will be found in almost every house. The landscape is flat and somewhat monotonous, and the field of the heavens has greater attractions there than in places which offer more variety of view. In the days in which I lived there the men of the community were mostly engaged in sea traffic of some sort and 'when my ship comes in' was a literal not symbolic expression.

Although Maria would one day gain greater notoriety than her father for her own work in astronomy, this early lesson in the relationship between science and daily life gave Maria a healthy respect for the work she did and for the notion that the truth came only through constant vigilance of the stars. She would one day write: "[I] was born of only ordinary capacity, but of extraordinary persistence."

And persistence was exactly what was called for in those early days of modern astronomy. By today's standards, with such devices as the Hubble Telescope and radio arrays, the tools that William used to teach Maria astronomy were crude and clumsy. Her first lessons about the nature of the solar system were taught through a model her father had built. The planets and the sun were made of wooden balls, and the orbits of the solar satellites were marked by ellipses drawn on the floor. This loose contraption took up the entire attic of the Mitchell home. The size, scope, and specific nature of this model gives some indication of the importance that the Mitchell parents placed on education, and especially astronomical education.

The empirical lessons she was taught on her rooftop were aided only by a sextant, a chronometer, and a small reflecting telescope — devices not much more complex than the wooden model of the solar system in her attic. From such humble beginnings, Maria would one day prove her genius to the world and would be honored by a king.

When Maria was in her early teens, her father had to give up his private school to take a more lucrative job as the principal officer of the Pacific Bank. The Mitchell family moved into housing provided by the bank on its premises. Maria's father took the opportunity to construct a new observatory for his astronomical studies. He placed it on top of the Pacific Bank and added more sophisticated instruments, making this early "Mitchell Observatory" the center of astronomical observation on the island.

Since her father's school was now defunct, Maria was required to complete her education elsewhere. She enrolled at Cyrus Pierce's School for Young Ladies. Cyrus Pierce was one of the first people outside of Maria's own family to recognize the acuity and expanse of Maria's mind. He saw that she had a facility and attraction to things mathematical, and he encouraged her in these areas. More than that, Pierce perceived a genius in the making. He would one day write that he saw in her "the quality of self-discipline together with the rare insight which makes the difference between a creative life and the prosaic existence of a mere fact collector." Maria's career would not disappoint this prophecy.

By age sixteen, Maria had completed her studies at the Pierce School. This was also the end of her formal education. At the time, there was only one college that accepted women — Oberlin College in Ohio. Maria, however, did not want to give up her family, her community, and her study of the stars from her father's observatory. Instead, she accepted an offer to teach at the Pierce School. She worked there for a year and then, at the age of seventeen, she followed her father's example and founded her own school. She rented out a small room, put up advertisements, and opened shop in 1835. Like her father, Maria was an unconventional teacher. Classes took place at irregular times. Sometimes students would be called to school before the dawn to observe the morning habits of birds, or class would be extended late into the evening so students could be taught astronomy through direct observation of the stars. The school, however, lasted only a year.

In 1836, Maria was offered the position of librarian at the Nantucket Athenaeum. It was here that she would "complete" her education. The library was only open to the public in the afternoons and on Saturdays, so Maria had many quiet hours alone with the books. She took this opportunity to continue her intellectual endeavors and to influence the budding minds of the Nantucket school children who frequented the library. Although she would later be the recipient of three honorary graduate degrees, Maria herself attained higher education only through her own course of study. After leaving the Pierce School, she became a true autodidact. At the Athenaeum, she read and closely studied such works as Bridge's Conic Sections, Hutton's Mathematics, Bowditch's Practical Navigator, and Gauss's Theoria Motus Coporeum Coelestium, all in pursuit of greater and more complete knowledge of celestial phenomenon. In addition, she continued to educate the minds of Nantucket youth. As librarian, she was privy to the reading habits of the schoolchildren who used the Athenaeum. If she saw them reading books she deemed inappropriate or intellectually useless, she would conveniently misplace these books and guide the children towards volumes she believed would increase their knowledge and excite their curiosity about the nature of the world around them.

All this time, Maria continued to assist her father with his astronomy, as well as conduct investigations of her own from her father's roof-top observatory. She would work all day in the library, and then make her way home to spend the evening diligently studying the stars. It was during one of her nights of solo observations that Maria saw a fuzzy dot near the North Star. This fuzzy dot would catapult her to international fame and recognition.

On October 1, 1847, Maria's father was hosting a small dinner party for friends and colleagues. Maria, never one to shirk her study of the heavenly orbs, stole away from the festivities to take advantage of the evening's particularly clear skies. She saw through the roof-top telescope a small, fuzzy light just above the North Star. From her years of recording her observations and studying celestial maps, Maria knew that there was no star at this location. She watched this fuzzy light for a long while before deciding it was no star, but rather an undiscovered comet. She could hardly believe her own conclusion. She ran down to the party and dragged her father to the telescope. He took one look through the telescope, then turned to his daughter and told her that he believed she was right. The self-taught, lady astronomer of Nantucket had discovered the world's first comet visible only through a telescope.

At the time, there was a world-wide race to discover this elusive species of astronomical phenomenon, the telescopic comet. The King of Denmark had a standing offer of a national medal for the first person to discover such an object. Maria's father wrote immediately to William Cranch Bond at the Harvard Observatory to inform him of Maria's discovery. But the technology of the time would again prove an obstacle to Maria's success. Nantucket, being a nineteenth-century island community, did not have daily mail service to the mainland, so it took several days for the announcement to reach Bond at Harvard. Furthermore, there was at that time no trans-Atlantic cable connecting America with Europe, so it took even longer for news of Maria's discovery to reach Denmark. In the meantime, the comet was observed during the subsequent, intervening days by four European astronomers, all of whom laid claim to the King of Denmark's medal.

It took over a year to sort out the five claims to the discovery of this first telescopic comet. But finally, Maria received word from Denmark that she had been recognized as having priority in the discovery. She was awarded the medal, and the comet was dubbed "Comet Mitchell 1847VI" to honor her discovery. From this point on, Maria would be recognized for her astronomical genius not only in the small community of Nantucket, but throughout the world.

Maria began to receive letters of congratulations and support from scientists around the world, and tourists and astronomers alike made pilgrimages to Nantucket to see the "town librarian" who had discovered a small, fiery needle in a celestial haystack. The famous American novelist Herman Melville wrote of one of his visits to Nantucket that he "passed the evening with Mr. Mitchell, the astronomer, and his celebrated daughter, the discoverer of comets." Maria was lauded by numerous magazine articles discussing her discovery and her life. And news of her discovery led to a lifelong friendship with Joseph Henry, the physicist who directed the newly founded Smithsonian Institute in Washington, D.C. Despite all this fan-fare, she continued in her position as librarian of the Athenaeum. But Maria's life was quickly becoming more complex.

In 1848, Maria Mitchell was elected the first female member of the American Academy of Arts and Sciences, an honor also bestowed on her by the Association for the Advancement of Science in 1850. Suddenly, Maria was the first professional female astronomer in America. Because of her success in studying the heavens, Maria was offered a paying position by the U.S. Nautical Almanac Office to compute positional tables of the movements of Venus in 1849. She would hold this post for nineteen years. She also began to attend astronomy meetings throughout America.

In 1856, Maria's life took a major turn. General Swift, a wealthy Chicago businessman, offered Maria a substantial amount to accompany his daughter as a chaperone on a trip to the South and to Europe. Maria, not one to waste any moment of her life, took her Almanac work with her, as well as letters of introduction from American scientists, in the hopes that she could gain access to some of the world-famous observatories of Europe. In London, she visited the Greenwich Observatory, and it was at this juncture that her young ward was recalled early to the States. Maria continued on to France alone where she met the writer Nathaniel Hawthorne, whose family accompanied her to Rome. It was in Rome that Maria would realize the tenuous position that a female scientist occupied in nineteenth-century society. Maria wanted to visit the Vatican Observatory, but the Catholic hierarchy did not permit women in the observatory. Through a great deal of lobbying, negotiation, and argument, Maria was finally allowed to visit the observatory, but only in the daytime. Although she was celebrated worldwide and carried with her letters of introduction from some of the finest scientists in America, Maria Mitchell was not allowed to observe the stars through the Pope's telescope because she was a woman.

In 1861, after Maria returned from her European travels, her mother died. She moved with her father to Lynn, Massachusetts where one of the other Mitchell daughters lived. There, she continued her work for the Almanac and her general study of the stars. In 1865 came the crowning glory of her career. A wealthy and enlightened man, Matthew Vassar, intended to open the now-famous Vassar College for women. This idea was rare for the day, being only the second women's college in America, and it was made even more rare by Vassar's intention to hire women as well as men as professors. He offered Maria the dual position of Professor of Astronomy and Director of the Observatory. The appointment was not without resistance, however, and trouble arose in Vassar's negotiations with the college board. Just as it was believed that the "over-education" of women would destroy their health, so it was believed that women working outside the home would make them pale and sickly. But Vassar was a persuasive and unstoppable man, and he pushed through Maria's appointment against all argument. She held the position for 23 years.

While at Vassar, Maria's astronomy classes were considered the favorite among students. She was exciting and enthusiastic and infused her students with a hunger for knowledge and accurate study. She achieved this celebrity by continuing her unconventional teaching practices at Vassar. She slept in the same dormitory building as the students, and would often rouse them in the middle of a bitterly cold night to observe a meteor shower. Afterwards, she would usher them into her quarters and they would sit around a fire, drink coffee, and discuss astronomy.

Maria also started a tradition that continues to this day at Vassar — Dome Parties. On nights when the sky was too obscured by clouds to perform any useful observations, Maria would invite the students to the observatory for socializing. She would stand at the entrance and greet each student as they arrived. When all were assembled, Maria would pass out little ribboned scrolls, one to each student. Each scroll had a little poem on it which Maria had written especially for that student, and they would go around the room reading each person's poem in turn. But above all, Maria taught her students the sense of dedication to accuracy and careful observation that she had been taught by her father so many years before on the rooftop of her family home.

Though she was by far the most popular professor at the newly-founded college, Maria still faced many problems common to women in academia, even to this day. She was paid only one-third the salary of the male professors at Vassar, and she was constantly subjected to the sexist axiom that women were unsuited to mathematical and scientific pursuits. Maria used the bases of these sexist beliefs to argue against their own conclusions:

The perceptive faculties of women [are] more acute than those of men. [Women would] perceive the size, form and color of an object more readily and would catch an impression more quickly. The training of girls (bad as it is) leads them to develop these faculties. The fine needlework and the embroidery teach them to measure small spaces. The same delicacy of eye and touch is needed to bisect the image of a star by a spider's web, as to piece delicate muslin with a fine needle. The small fingers too come into play with a better adaptation to delicate micrometer screws.

But she did more for the advancement of women than just make fine arguments and study the stars. She was an integral member of the burgeoning movement of suffragists and women's rights activists that was developing in late nineteenth-century America. She joined such luminaries as Susan B. Anthony in championing a woman's rights to vote, own property, and receive the same type of education and opportunities offered to men. To this end, Maria helped found the Association for the Advancement of Women in 1873. She served as the Association's president for two years and as chair of the Association's science committee until her death.

On Christmas Day, 1888, after serving as the first female professor of astronomy, and after a long distinguished career as the first professional female astronomer in America, Maria retired to Lynn, Massachusetts to spend the remainder of her days with family. She died a year later.

Some have argued that Maria Mitchell's scientific work was not of lasting importance. Though she recorded, catalogued, and calculated astronomical phenomena with unending diligence and care, she contributed nothing to astronomical theory, and her decades of data collection are long since outdated by the measurements of our modern, more refined equipment. With the exception of her discovery of Comet Mitchell, she never shook the foundations of the celestial science. But Maria's most important contributions were not so much to the body of scientific knowledge as they were to the cause of the advancement of women both in society and science. Through her unfailing spirit and diligence, Maria showed that a little girl from Nantucket, or anywhere, had the ability and intellect to unlock and understand the mysteries of the stars.

Chapter 2

෩෬

Ellen Henrietta Swallow Richards

E llen Henrietta Swallow was born into the harsh environment of a small, pre-Civil War New England farm. By all accounts, her life was set to follow one of two destinies: to become a skilled wife, or to become a skilled spinster. But Ellen, growing up on the farm, helping her father with chores, and taking long walks through the stony hills cut with brooks which marked the landscape of her childhood home, learned to have a strong mind in place of a strong body. She sought out a destiny unavailable to most women of the time. Armed with a sharp intellect and a rapport with nature developed in her bucolic childhood, Ellen Swallow would grow to become one of the pioneers of modern science. Not only would she break through various academic glass ceilings during her life, but this woman, whose life straddled two centuries, would become the first American woman to found an entire branch of science; a science that would completely alter the way Americans, and the world, viewed the health and safety of their public spaces and their homes.

Ellen Henrietta Swallow was born to Peter and Fanny Swallow on December 3, 1842 in the town of Dunstable, Massachusetts. It was a small town covering only sixteen miles of land, and was home to about five hundred inhabitants. The Swallows were hard-working citizens of a

Source: The MIT Museum, Cambridge, MA

young, pioneering country that was over two decades away from addressing its own form of tyranny during the Civil War, and was just moving past the memory of the violent movement for independence. Peter was a descendant from a Revolutionary soldier who was buried near the Dunstable farm. Ancestors on both sides of the Swallow family had immigrated to America in the mid-1660s. Members of Ellen's family forged through the harsh landscape of New England, making their way past rocky fields to settle finally in New Ipswich, New Hampshire. It was in this town that Ellen's parents first met. They were both students at the Ipswich Academy, and this rare opportunity enjoyed by both parents (to be formally educated in a time long before mandatory public education) would come to exert a strong influence on the life of young Ellen. Her parents' belief in a good, formal education for their child would provide her with the encouragement and intellectual foundation she would need to fulfill her own revolutionary destiny as one of the early greats of American science.

Both Peter and Fanny were schoolteachers before Ellen was born. But her father had gone back to farming by the time she was born, and Ellen was introduced to the hard life of New England farm-work. In addition to her father's farming, the family also earned money from Fanny's school teaching. But Fanny was often ill, and that source of income was irregular. The situation worsened after Ellen was born and Fanny's health deteriorated, leaving her bedridden more often than not. To compound matters, Ellen herself showed an early propensity to sickness, which her family and neighbors presumed to be inherited from her mother. Even the family doctor, a frequent guest of the ailing Swallow household, had little to offer in the way of hope. Medical knowledge in the nineteenth century was not the precise science of today. Diagnosing her generally to be in "poor health," Ellen's country doctor prescribed good food, fresh air, and plenty of sunshine for his young patient. This prescription would provide Ellen with the excuse and opportunity to explore nature in ways that would have been denied her had she been healthier. Under normal circumstances, Ellen would have been more confined to the home, learning the skills that would make her a good wife: cooking, cleaning, and embroidering.

Instead, Ellen explored the natural surroundings in Dunstable. When not helping her father pitch hay, drive a wagon, or herd the cows, and she could escape the domestic lessons and chores, Ellen would wander through the meadows, hills, and streams of her country environment.

She breathed the fresh air, sat beside a bubbling brook, and let her ever-acute mind expand in the surroundings that would one day inspire her to write: "Air and Water are Food."

Ellen's mother, Fanny, was an extremely astute and progressive woman for the time. She and Ellen's father provided home-schooling for their daughter because neither parent believed the local, one-room schoolhouse offered a decent education. Ellen's parents taught her mathematics, writing, literature, history, and logic. They taught their daughter in an unconventional way by encouraging her to make connections, draw conclusions, and understand her relationship to the world around her. These skills provided Ellen with a strong foundation for the great scientific achievements in her life.

But Fanny was concerned that her daughter would become too much of a "tomboy," and it would ruin her chance at marriage, a rite of passage considered the most important step in a woman's life. Although Fanny accepted the health benefits of Ellen's many outdoor activities, she could not accept her daughter milking cows because she was afraid it would mar Ellen's dainty hands. Thus, Ellen also became proficient at "women's work." She learned to bake, sew, and clean, and even won ribbons at the county fairs for her baking and embroidery. But as Maria Mitchell, one of her future mentors and the first female astronomer, would point out, any mind capable of understanding the intricacies of embroidery was capable of understanding the intricacies of science.

Over time, Ellen overcame her many illnesses. Her time outdoors and the constant mental stimulation and encouragement of her parents helped her regain her health. By her late teenage years, Ellen had become a robust young woman ready to take on the world of learning and science, which had been generally barred to women.

Interested in fostering their child's budding intellect, the Swallows left the farm and moved to Westford, a nearby town that had an academy at which Ellen's parents believed she could find a quality education. Her father took what little money the family earned from the sale of the farm and opened a small general store. Like most of his ventures, the store would be neither a business success or failure, but would provide for the family at a slightly higher than hand-to-mouth level.

Though now living a more urban lifestyle, and enrolled in a course of formal education at the Westford Academy, Ellen's days were still full of domestic responsibilities. She continued to bear the burden of household duties her invalid mother could not perform, and she helped out at her father's store both early in the morning unpacking barrels and stocking bins and shelves and in the afternoons working as a store clerk. By all accounts, Ellen was a charming young woman, even a little impish and mischievous with her father's customers. It was during this time that she began to study, in an informal way, the knowledge and habits that people had about food and health, areas in which Ellen would pioneer new ways of thinking. There was an ongoing debate at the time as to whether saleratus or baking powder made for better baking. Having stocked the bins herself, Ellen knew that the two ingredients were identical and she noted with fascination, and a bit of disapproval, how people were ignorant of the substances they put in their bodies. It was not only the food people ate, but also the air they breathed that concerned Ellen. Once, to the great chagrin of the customers, Ellen asked a group of men who had just purchased a few ounces of tobacco to leave the store before lighting their pipes because she believed the polluted air was bad for everyone's health.

At the Academy, Ellen was being provided with the knowledge and intellectual skills that would later turn her informal observations into a lifetime's work. Her headmasters were mostly young graduates from Harvard, and they taught her along classical lines. She learned Latin, the foundation of most formal education of the time, and excelled to the point where she was allowed to tackle both French and German. She also began to demonstrate her talent in mathematics, and displayed a supremely logical mind capable of great feats of organization and understanding.

During this time, Ellen continued her relationship with nature begun on the farm. She wandered into the nearby countryside to collect flowers and fossils, all of which she meticulously cataloged and classified in her diaries and letters. It was this devotion to understanding nature's relationship to humanity, a great intellect, and a belief in hard work that would be the foundation of Ellen's career as a pioneer of modern science.

Ellen graduated from Westford Academy in 1864. At that time, her parents decided to close shop in Westford and move to the larger town of Littleton, where Peter opened a larger store with a post office substation and gave it to Ellen to run. She worked there for a year and then accepted a teaching position in Worcester, Massachusetts. It was during this time that Ellen would learn the value of a free and independent life. She was now well into the age of marriage, but her letters to family members displayed a growing distrust of that particular social institution. To her mother, Ellen wrote: "There is no possibility of your dreams proving true at the present, for the young or old gentleman has not yet made his appearance who can entice me away from my free and independent life." Her observations of married life indicated that she was generally disgusted with the whole affair. She wrote: "I know of no lady with whom I would exchange places. The gentleman whom I think the most of and who comes the nearest to my ideal . . . does not treat his wife as I wish to be treated . . . I often tell him we could not live together . . . more than a week." She also observed: "Girls don't get behind the scenes as I have, or they could not get up such an enthusiasm for married life." And as for children: "The world will be peopled without my help." Instead, Ellen continued her intellectual pursuits that would help her better understand her world and contribute something to it.

But her dreams were to be temporarily deferred, and her faith in them would have to provide her strength through a dark period. Illness again overcame her mother, and Ellen was recalled to Littleton. Taken from her independent life and placed suddenly back in the dreary world of domestic duties, Ellen became depressed. Nearly every day for the next two years, she recorded feelings of exhaustion with the small, simple entry: "Tired." In later life she would refer to these two years as "purgatory."

But in 1868, events in the larger world opened up an unforeseen opportunity for Ellen. Matthew Vassar, a rebellious and wealthy entrepreneur, opened his experimental college in 1865. Although there were a smattering of schools in the Midwest that offered some opportunity for women to enter higher education, Vassar was the first institution devoted to providing women with a college education. It was an idea that shocked and threatened most of the country, since social convention still dictated that women had only limited intellectual capabilities, and that any pursuit of higher education was both unethical and sinful because it took women from their proper duties at home. Ellen applied to Vassar and was admitted to the junior level because of the high marks she received on the entrance exam. Her experiences at the college brought together her personality and intellect into a solid and focused whole.

At Vassar, she studied all areas of science, including anatomy, biology, astronomy, and chemistry. As her own knowledge grew, and as she came into contact with powerful women such as the famous astronomer Maria Mitchell, Ellen became more aware and more concerned about the oppressed role of women in society. During this time she realized her desire to pioneer in expanding women's boundaries. She believed that education was the battleground on which this war should be fought, and her lifelong work in academia would allow her to fight for both better public health standards, and the rights of women to learn and contribute to the knowledge of their world.

Ellen's primary scientific interests were astronomy and chemistry. She chose to focus on chemistry. Ellen, herself, had experienced in childhood the health benefits provided by proper sanitary conditions, such as clean air and water, and she came to believe that she could do more for the world by studying the chemistry of everyday substances, such as water and food, and developing an understanding of the relationship between these substances and health, than she could by studying the stars. Ellen received her B.A. from Vassar in 1870. On the final day of classes, Maria Mitchell said to Ellen, "You will make valuable discoveries in your life."

At first, Ellen's professional goals were thwarted. She wanted to apply her knowledge of chemistry to real-world problems and, to that end, applied to various chemical firms in the Northeast. All of them rejected her, explaining that the world of commercial chemistry offered no opportunities for women. One letter, however, offered her some hope. It suggested that she look into the Massachusetts Institute of Technology if she wished to continue her work in chemistry. MIT was only five years old at the time, but was already earning a reputation as a hotbed of scientific and technological learning. She wrote the president of MIT to ask if they would accept women. She described her work under Maria Mitchell and the chemist Dr. Farrand at Vassar. MIT's president, Dr. Runkle, happened to be a close friend and colleague of both Mitchell and Farrand, and although MIT had a policy of not admitting women, Dr. Runkle decided to make an exception for Ellen. She was admitted as a special student in 1871. In order to preempt any possible disaster from this experiment, the board decided that Ellen would not be charged tuition, so they could claim she was not an official student if the experiment proved unsuccessful. Although much of the work she did in the laboratories of MIT was menial (the male professors and students directed her to clean and organize the labs), Ellen was one of the very few women afforded access to the best labs and equipment of the time. She was one of MIT's most successful students, and graduated in 1873 with a Bachelor of Science degree. Two years later, having been retained as a staff worker at MIT, she married a young professor of mining engineering, Dr. Robert Richards. Although Ellen had previously rejected marriage, she acquiesced because in Dr. Richards she found the only type of husband she could accept — a husband that supported her own intellectual endeavors and who treated her as an equal in both matters of science and matters of home life. In fact, it is due in great part to her husband that the history of Ellen Swallow Richard's work has been preserved.

During the two years between her graduation and her marriage, Ellen was involved in one of the earliest attempts to create public health standards. The Massachusetts State Board of Health had begun a project to evaluate the purity of the public water supplies. They hired Dr. William Nichols of MIT to oversee the project, and he chose Ellen as his assistant. Ellen conducted and analyzed countless tests on water samples from around the state, and her dedication and accuracy earned her a commendation in Dr. Nichols' final report to the Board of Health. When the project ended, Ellen was hired on to similar projects in the growing field of chemical analysis for commercial and industrial purposes. She studied the chemistry of oils for fire insurance companies and food for the State Board of Health.

During this time she also increased her social activism. She made contact with the growing number of women's associations of the time and, with their support, she convinced MIT to expand the experiment it had begun with her. She convinced the board to open the Women's Laboratory, where women could come to receive high-level scientific training with proper equipment and experienced professors. This new experiment was still considered just that, however. The female students were not considered full members of the university, just as Ellen had not been a "real student." Ellen worked hard to maintain the Women's Laboratory, although she was never accorded a title, nor was she paid to operate the lab. But in just a few short years, her efforts and the success of the female students proved so overwhelming that MIT dismantled the separatist laboratory and began accepting women as full and equal students.

Thirteen years after completing the preliminary water analyses for the Board of Health, Dr. Nichols was again contacted to conduct a more intensive study of the drinking water supply for the state. The Board was interested in MIT's newly opened laboratory devoted to sanitary chemistry, to which Ellen had been appointed as head assistant, earning her the honor of being the first female faculty member of MIT. As the head lab assistant, Ellen studied the sanitation of the public water supply with vigor and accuracy. She made thousands upon thousands of analyses to determine the chemical content of various water tables around the state. Through her work she developed the world's first ever Normal Chlorine Map, a system by which the purity of any local water supply could be judged and regulated.

Ellen's most important scientific achievements, however, were yet to come and they would occupy the rest of her life. Throughout her life and career, Ellen had been concerned with health and sanitation standards, and paid particular attention to the effects of impure air, water, and food on the body. She now turned her mind and chemical expertise on the primary source of these basic nourishments: the home. It is for her work in this area that she is considered to have been the founder of the science of Home Economics, or Domestic Science. It began with a simple question she posed to a professor at MIT who once asked her what good chemistry would do for a woman in the kitchen. She responded: "Well, why shouldn't chemistry be applied in the home?" She believed that chemistry specifically, and the scientific method in general, could improve the unhealthy state of the American home.

She began in her own home. She and her husband developed efficient systems in their household that addressed both labor and health issues. They replaced carpets with area rugs, which were easier to keep clean, and replaced heavy drapes, which gathered dust and kept out light, with sheer curtains, which brightened rooms and were more easily removed for cleaning. They also experimented with the effects of diet on the body and the mind, and developed a menu that called for only moderate meat consumption, with an emphasis on fresh water, fruits, and vegetables.

Ellen even attempted to implement these health standards on a wide scale in Boston. At the time, there was no federal Food and Drug Administration keeping track of the food products sold. Consequently, Americans suffered at the hand of food dealers who indiscriminately put poisonous preservatives in their products, or misrepresented their contents. One attempt to provide better standards that met with failure was a public kitchen at which the poor could procure sanitary and healthy food. But the citizenry did not accept someone telling them what they should and should not eat. Ellen nonetheless forged onward and established a similar campaign in Boston's public schools. Here she instituted a practice of providing healthy and nourishing meals for the children, which were free of poisons, spoilage, and non-nutritional bulk.

During this time Ellen was hired by MIT to give lectures and lessons on sanitary food conditions. Eventually, her lectures became a requirement for all MIT students. In addition, she was hired to design a model home for working people which was displayed at the Chicago World's Fair. Her crowning glory and the entity representing all her efforts both great and small, was the founding of the American Home Economics Association. Through this organization, for which she served as the first president, Ellen disseminated information on better health standards for the world.

In her life, Ellen Swallow Richards rose above gender discrimination to become a scientific pioneer. She made her dream of a better, healthier life the goal of her scientific work and, eventually, the common goal of an unwilling society. She reached heights thought unattainable for women of her era, although she was, in the end, denied certain earned achievements, such as a full professorship at MIT or a Ph.D.. But she did expand the boundaries that confined women, and offered a ray of hope for those who would follow her into the halls of science and academia. She died quietly, with her husband by her side, in her Boston home on March 30, 1911.

Chapter 3

෩ඏ

Marie Sklodowska Curie

Bundled in all her clothes and a single coverlet, she pulled a chair on top of her, hoping the weight would provide the illusion of heat. Sleep did not come easily in the unheated sixth floor garret. Before closing her eyes, she scribbled a few thoughts in her little gray notebook:

> Ah! how harshly the youth of the student passes,
> While all around her, with passions ever fresh,
> Other youths search for easy pleasures!
> And yet in solitude
> She lives, obscure and blessed,
> For in her cell she finds the ardor,
> That makes her heart immense.

Tormented by her intellectual ambition, she desired only to satisfy an unyielding hunger to explore the world of science. The "ardor that makes her heart immense" would eventually lead to majestic discoveries, and two Nobel Prizes. She was the determined little Polish girl who would become Marie Curie.

In 1867, she was born Marya Sklodowska (nicknamed Manya), the youngest of five children, in Warsaw, Poland. Her father, Wladislaw Sklodowska, was the under-inspector at the high school where he taught

Source: AIP Emilio Segrè Visual Archives, W. F. Meggers Collection

physics. Bronislawa Bojuska, Manya's mother, was the principal at the girl's school until the onset of tuberculosis. Fearing that she might transmit the disease to her children, Bronislawa became distant and unaffectionate toward her children. Manya was instead brought up in an intellectual atmosphere. It was not uncommon for the family to gather around the dining room table in the evening to recite poetry. As her daughter, Eve Curie, would recall: "Manya must have grown to imagine the universe as an immense school where there were only teachers and pupils and where only one ideal reigned: to learn."

By the time she was sixteen, Manya Sklodowska had already exhibited characteristics of greatness — she was the star pupil in Mlle. Sikorska's school, despite being two years younger than her classmates. Upon the completion of her secondary education at the Russian Lycee, she won a Gold Medal, just as her sister Bronya and brother Jozio had done. She graduated first in her class in every subject. A discerning student with a prodigious memory, Manya was fascinated by the instruments, tubes, scales, and mineral specimens in her father's workroom.

Marie desperately wanted to continue her studies after high school, but women were not admitted to the University of Warsaw. In fact, in an atmosphere of political intimidation and oppression, most young Poles could only get a university education abroad, as Poland was under Russian dominion at the time.

After graduation, Manya, physically exhausted from the strain of school, was sent to stay with relatives in the country for a year. Eve Curie would describe the stay there as one of her mother's happiest times:

> Many years later my mother sometimes evoked those happy days for me . . . I thanked the destiny which, before it dedicated this woman's austere and inexorable summons, had allowed her to follow by sleigh after the wildest *kuligs,* and to use up her shoes of russet leather in one night of dancing.

Returning home to Warsaw to stay with her father, Manya decided to give private lessons. She joined a "floating university," a group of sympathetic teachers who privately instructed young students. The floating university had both socialist and scholarly goals. It was also at this time that she and her sister, Bronya, began following an underground political movement among the "intellegentsia." They called themselves "positivists." Their goal was to build the intellectual capital of Poland.

Manya and Bronya yearned to study science and medicine in Paris. Manya concocted a plan to finance her sister's medical studies in Paris by working as a governess. They made an agreement that Bronya would reciprocate the support once she was well on her way. Manya worked as a governess for five relatively unhappy years until, in 1891, almost penniless, she gathered her belongings and headed to Paris herself.

She enrolled at the Faculty of Science at the Sorbonne. Now "Marie," she spent two long years working tirelessly, late into every night. Iron-willed and obsessed with perfection, Marie Sklodowska dedicated every waking hour (usually 20) to her studies. She became intoxicated by mathematics, physics, and chemistry. She was the number one student in her physics class and number two in her mathematics class. The Sorbonne took notice of Marie's astute mind and implacable character.

It was a time when she was battling poverty, but was proud of it. She recalled that although life was painful, it had a "real charm" and gave her a "precious sense of liberty and independence." It was no surprise to Bronya to find her sister anemic and malnourished in the small rented hovel. Although Marie had a rare internal fortitude, her body could not always keep up.

Marie had long ago resolved that love and marriage were not for her; she decided she would find intimacy in science. But then she met a man named Pierre Curie. He was a brilliant French scientist and the laboratory director of the Municipal School of Industrial Physics and Chemistry in Paris. He and his brother, Jacques, had discovered piezoelectricity while studying the physics of crystals. They had also invented an apparatus for making precise measurements of small quantities of electricity, called a piezoelectric quartz balance. Marie was not only struck by his genius, but also "by the expression of his clear gaze and by the slight appearance of carelessness in his lofty stature. [His] rather slow reflective words, his simplicity, and his smile, at once grave and young, inspired her confidence."

After much hesitation, having always wanted to return to work in Poland, she married him in 1895. Bronya's mother-in-law bought Marie's wedding dress. At Marie's insistence, the dress was a dark suit that could be used as a lab uniform as well. For their honeymoon, the newlyweds, in their modest style, took off on a pair of bicycles to roam the roads of France. Pierre and Marie enlarged their family with the birth of two daughters, Irene in 1887 and Eve in 1904.

Despite the new additions to the family, Marie continued to work full-time. Inspired by Henri Becquerel's discovery that uranium gave off a mysterious type of penetrating radiation, Madame Curie dedicated her dissertation research to exploring the source of the rays emitted by uranium salt (she was only one of two women in Europe working toward a doctorate degree). Her dissertation committee later declared her thesis, "Researches on Radioactive Substances," the greatest contribution ever made by a doctoral dissertation.

Her work on these "strange rays" proved to be so promising that Pierre Curie left his own work in physics to collaborate with his wife. In the words of Eve Curie, "two hearts beat together; two bodies were united; and two minds of genius learned to think together." Of this time in their lives, Marie Curie would later write: "We had no money, no laboratory, and no help . . . And yet it was in this miserable old shed that the best and happiest years of our life were spent, entirely consecrated to work."

Marie discovered that the actual strength of the rays emitted by such salts was dependent on the amount of uranium present. She thus became convinced that radiation was an atomic property. Examining a number of substances, she found that thorium and its compounds behaved in the same fashion as uranium. She referred to the power to emit rays as "radioactivity." While exploring pitchblende (the ores left over when uranium has been extracted), she came to the conclusion that a powerful radioactive substance existed in the minerals. In 1898, Marie Curie sent a preliminary note to the Academy of Sciences, announcing the possible presence of a radioactive element in pitchblende ores. It was the beginning of the Atomic Age.

The Curies predicted that the new element was present in only very minute quantities. Later they disclosed that the radioactivity existed only in certain parts of the ore. They soon discovered two new elements, resembling the chemical properties of bismuth. In July 1898, they announced the discovery of one of these elements, polonium, named after Marie's beloved homeland. In December of the same year they announced the discovery of another new element, radium.

Several dismayed scientists claimed that the new elements, polonium and radium, existed only in imperceptible traces in the substances they produced. The Curies thus set out to obtain these elements in their pure form in the unheated, ramshackle shed behind the Sorbonne School of Physics. After four years of physical and mental exertion, and after submitting over eight tons of pitchblende for chemical analysis, they managed to isolate one decigramme of pure radium metal. Marie calculated the atomic weight at 225. Radium was perhaps the most important element to be discovered since oxygen. In 1903, Marie Curie, her husband, and Henri Becquerel received the Nobel Prize for Physics for the discovery of radioactivity. Marie was the first woman to be so honored.

The unpretentious Curie was unaware of the prestige that was attached to Alfred Nobel's Prize. According to her daughter, Eve, she seemed unaffected by the fact that she was the first woman to win the Nobel Prize. In a letter to her brother on December 11, 1903, Marie wrote: "We have been given half of the Nobel Prize. I do not know exactly what that represents; I believe it is about sixty thousand francs." In the end, the Curies renounced all material profit from their discovery of radium. To patent their technique, Marie insisted, would be contrary to the scientific spirit.

The Curies' work in isolating radium had a significant impact on the study of radioactivity by others. Becquerel used a radium salt to demonstrate the similarity between the rays emitted and cathode rays. He also found that the radiation given off by polonium was much less penetrating than that from radium. Rutherford demonstrated that the rays emitted from uranium were of two kinds: alpha and beta rays. Radioactivity also became the primary technique for exploring the interior of the atom. The work of Pierre and Marie led scientists to alter significantly their ideas of matter.

In 1906, Pierre Curie, weakened by exposure to radiation, fell in front of a horsedrawn cart and was killed instantly. Marie's world suddenly collapsed. Eve Curie describes the effect of Pierre's death on her mother:

> The interior tumult that lacerated Marie, the nameless horror of her wandering ideas, were too virulent to be expressed in complaints or in confidences. From the moment when those three words, 'Pierre is dead,' reached her consciousness, a cape of solitude and secrecy fell upon her shoulders forever. Marie Curie on that day in April, became not only a widow, but at the same time a pitiful and incurable lonely woman.

Outwardly, Marie remained composed and automated, but privately, the devastation filled her entirely. The house where they had lived held too many memories, and so the Curie family left their home on the boulevard Kellerman and rented a house in Sceaux, where Pierre was buried.

In the years that followed Pierre's death, the doleful widow lost herself in her work. She spent countless hours in the laboratory. In 1908, she took over her husband's professorship at the Sorbonne, making her the first woman to hold such a post in the Sorbonne's 650-year history. She published a fundamental treatise on radioactivity in 1910 (*Traite de Radioactivite*). Shortly thereafter, she succeeded in isolating pure radium in the metallic state. She was also able to find a method for measuring the emanations from radium. Additionally, Marie formulated the first international standard of radium — 21.99 milligrams of pure radium chloride.

In 1911, she was awarded the Nobel Prize in Chemistry for the isolation of pure radium, thereby becoming the first person to receive two Nobel awards. The president of the Swedish Academy acclaimed that the second award was proof of the importance that the Academy attached to her discoveries.

In 1914, the Sorbonne and the Pasteur Institute established an institute in honor of Marie and Pierre Curie. On Pierre Curie Avenue at the Institute of Radium, Marie presided over the laboratory of radioactivity and an eminent physician, Claude Regaud, headed the laboratory for biological research and Curietherapy (radiation therapy).

With a world war looming, Marie quickly secured her one gram of radium in a bank vault and set out to contribute to the national defense. Curie, characterized as "all aflame," toured the front line with her X-ray vans, known as "little Curies," and along with 150 other French recruits, including her daughter Irene, examined over a million wounded men. In addition to equipping the cars, Madame Curie installed 200 radiological rooms. She requested that the money from her second Nobel Prize be turned into war bonds and even asked that her medals be melted down, but the Bank of France refused. Marie Curie was undoubtedly a passionate humanitarian.

Marie certainly did not expect the French government to decorate her with medals for her heroic war work. But according to Eve Curie, her mother was disheartened that her adopted country would not purchase a second gram of radium in order to further the research that promised life-saving benefits.

Interviewing Madame Curie at the Radium Institute in 1920, Mrs. William Brown Meloney, a wealthy American magazine editor, asked Marie Curie what she wanted most. Marie responded that she wanted a gram of radium to continue her research. Mrs. Meloney took it upon herself to solicit donations from American women to aid the great scientist to further contribute to the world's fund of knowledge. Within a year, Marie Curie was invited to the United States to accept the one gram of radium from President Warren G. Harding. A gala tour was arranged and Dr. Curie accepted honorary degrees from twenty universities before attending a reception at the White House. Marie would call on Mrs. Meloney once more to help fund the research of cancer treatment at the Radium Institute in Warsaw that was established in 1925.

Dr. Curie had the satisfaction of knowing that her life-time contributions were instrumental in treating cancer. Marie herself would succumb to cancer after years of exposure to radium. She dedicated her life to radium, and radium took her life away. Eve wrote:

> She was on that last day just as gentle, stubborn, timid and curious about all things as in the days of her obscure beginnings. A hard and long and dazzling career had not succeeded in making her greater or less, in sanctifying or debasing her . . . I should have liked the gifts of a writer to tell of this eternal student — of whom Einstein said: "Marie Curie is, of all celebrated beings, the only one whom fame has not corrupted" — passing like a stranger across her own life, intact, natural and very nearly unaware of her astonishing destiny.

On July 4, 1934, Marie Curie's coffin was buried on top of her husband's at the cemetery in Sceaux, France.

Although Marie was widely recognized for her discovery of radium and for laying the groundwork for modern nuclear physics, she was not always applauded. At a time when no woman had made any significant contribution to science, she was discouraged as often as she was praised. While being considered for membership to the prestigious French Academy of Science, Marie was the target of a malicious slander campaign. She was harassed by anonymous letters and phone calls. It caused Marie to retreat in solitude, leaving her on the brink of a nervous breakdown on several occasions. The Academy rejected her for membership, claiming that women could not be part of the Institute of France (they appointed the first woman in 1979). Even as late as 1971, at the annual meeting of the American Physical Society, a well-known male physicist stated: "If I had been married to Pierre Curie, *I* would have been Marie Curie."

Not only was she a woman, she was also a foreigner. France, her adopted country, never embraced Marie Curie as its own unless she was being honored with a prestigious award. It was not uncommon for the xenophobic French Press to hurl insults at Marie, especially after the 1911 scandal, in which Marie befriended Paul Langevin, a gifted and influential French physicist, and a married man. When Langevin rented two rooms on the Rue du Banquier, a ten minute walk from Curie's lab, she visited him daily. Tabloids and newspapers accused the two of being lovers, which led to crowds of people around Marie's home calling out: "Husband stealer" and "Get the foreign woman out." Some even resorted to throwing stones at her home. Whatever the relationship, the social climate of the day ended it.

For a deeply reserved and private woman who always appeared composed, the distractions of fame did not rest well with Marie. As Eve writes: "She did not know how to be famous." Even in her last words, she cried to be left in peace. Her happiest days were not accepting Nobel Prizes, touring the United States, or being decorated with honors; they were in the laboratory. In a letter dated September 1927 to her sister Bronya, Marie writes:

> Sometimes my courage fails me and I think I ought to stop working, live in the country and devote myself to gardening. But I am held by a thousand bonds, and I don't know when I shall be able to arrange things otherwise. *Nor do I know whether, even by writing scientific books, I could live without the laboratory.*

In the laboratory, Marie Curie found comfort. And it was there that she changed the world forever.

Chapter 4

ৰ০ભ

Alice Hamilton

The wild and unpredictable antics of the Mad Hatter in Lewis Carroll's *Alice in Wonderland* have frightened children of all ages. But few readers realize that the term "Mad Hatter" originated in hat factories during the Industrial Revolution. The discovery of electricity, coupled with the attempt to connect the United States with railroads and steamships, resulted in a time of rapid growth. Immigrants and citizens in a lower socio-economic class found work in the new industries and factories. These factories, however, were using poisonous chemicals to produce their goods, which caused many Americans to contract diseases and even die. Due to prolonged exposure to mercury nitrate (a deadly chemical), for example, the makers of felt hats grew extremely irritable and their limbs would tremble, hence the term "mad hatter." Conditions like this existed in hundreds of factories, but the workers did not complain as they feared they would lose their only source of income. At the time, there were no unions, no workman's compensation laws, and most importantly, no proof that deadly chemicals were being used in the workplace — that is, until Alice Hamilton changed our nation. She became America's foremost authority on industrial diseases. Through her tireless research and relentless investigations, she catalogued hundreds

Source: The Schlesinger Library, Radcliffe College

of poisons used in industry and linked these poisons to both disease and death. Her efforts led to the passage of America's first workman's compensation laws and forever changed the way America treats its employees.

Alice Hamilton was born into a privileged, charitable, and religious family in February 1869. She grew up on the family estate in Fort Wayne, Indiana interacting only with her sisters and cousins. All of the Hamilton children were schooled at home and the family rarely interacted with outsiders. This seclusion, however, led Alice to develop a rich inner-life. Through games with her cousins, she developed a sense of humor and adventure. The family servants taught her different languages and her father, a Princeton graduate, insisted that the girls pursue a variety of intellectual subjects. Indeed, being intellectual was a family requirement. Children of the Hamilton family could not assert a belief or point of view without having a strong argument with evidence to back it up. This instilled in Alice a strong sense of ambition and purpose, but it also gave her an underlying fear that she might someday fail and look upon her life with regret.

At the age of seventeen, Alice carried on the family tradition of attending the prestigious Miss Porter's school in Connecticut. After graduating, Alice's decision to study medicine shocked her family. At the time, women were supposed to become homemakers or teachers. But Alice's need to have personal liberty and be of use to society was too great to respect tradition. Alice believed that, as a doctor, she would be able to go anywhere she pleased — to far-off lands or city slums — and be sure that she could be of use. In addition, she would not be tied down to a school as a teacher or have to suffer a superior as nurses do. Her family objected to this choice, but Alice was determined to prove herself worthy. She enrolled in the Fort Wayne College of Medicine to make up for her deficiencies in science, a discipline her family's home-schooling largely overlooked. Through her diligent studies, she was accepted into the University of Michigan's medical program at the age of twenty three.

It was at the University of Michigan that Alice developed a fascination for the human cell, the basic building block of life. What caused "normal" cells to become diseased? Why did healthy cells sometimes die? Even today, these questions are still being asked by scientists, as they are fundamental to the understanding and elimination of disease. These questions fascinated Alice, and at the University of Michigan she decided to specialize in pathology and dedicate the rest of her life to studying disease.

One year later, she received her MD from the University and became a full-fledged doctor, not an easy task for a woman in 1893. Eager to begin her new life as both a scientist and a working doctor, Alice took an internship at the Hospital for Women and Children in Minneapolis. The internship frustrated Alice, who approached her scientific research with a profound sense of integrity. Not only did she find herself overworked, but her lab equipment was lacking and the methods of her fellow doctors were "unscientific." Hoping to find better treatment for patients and better working conditions, Alice accepted an offer to intern at the Hospital for Women and Children outside of Boston and quickly transferred.

The conditions in Boston weren't much better, which frustrated Alice even more. Although she had promised the hospital her services and was under contract, Alice believed that the hospital had failed to deliver on its promise of providing a good experience. Fortunately, the internship in Boston at least provided Alice with a sense of adventure. Most of her time was spent visiting poor and impoverished patients in their homes in Boston's slums and ghettos. Alice, who had grown up on her wealthy family's beautiful estate, was finally exposed to a side of the world that she had only heard about as a child. Alice saw first-hand the living conditions of our nation's forgotten poor and the diseases they contracted. Speaking with and caring for these patients had a profound effect on Alice. She could see clearly where she was needed in the world, but she also learned quickly that she did not want the responsibility of caring for individual patients. Although Alice was compassionate and wanted to help the underprivileged, watching patients die and families grieving over the loss of a loved one was unbearable for her. In a letter to her cousin Agnes, with whom she frequently corresponded, she described the death of a young woman under her care: "I can not tell you what a terrible time that was . . . On Friday she began to sink and at noon we thought she was steadying. And my dear, the heart-rending scene! All the worse because [the family was] so quiet and obeyed my slightest word so implicitly . . . I thought I could not stand another minute of it."

Knowing she did not want to be a traditional doctor, Alice was faced with the daunting task of finding a way to combine her love of pathology with her need for social work. Since there were no existing opportunities, Alice decided to continue her studies in Germany, which was the world's leading training ground for scientists of pathology. Alice was in Fort

Wayne preparing for her trip when she got word that the famous American social worker, Jane Addams, was giving a lecture in her home town. Jane Addams ran a settlement house in the Chicago slums, called the Hull House. Many people who wished to help the underprivileged lived at Hull House and set out to change the world. Alice heard Jane Addams speak and soon realized that she and Jane shared the same vision of public service and contribution. From that day, Alice knew that someday she would live at Hull House and somehow use her knowledge of pathology to help mankind.

Alice continued with her trip to Europe, however, where she was allowed to study bacteriology and pathology while attending the University of Leipzig and the University of Munich, but only on the condition she make herself inconspicuous. Even though she was an American doctor, she was officially regarded as invisible in the classroom and was forced to sit in the back corner of the lecture hall because she was a woman. Sadly, even after enduring this type of treatment, Alice did not learn anything she didn't already know. Germany's militarism, anti-Semitism, and sexism disgusted Alice, who returned to the United States disenchanted and disheartened.

By this time, Alice had developed herself into one of the top authorities on pathology. But she still couldn't find a job. What would she do for employment? How could she find a way to create a better society? Her prayers were answered when she received a position at the Women's Medical College at Northwestern University in Chicago. Alice thought that she could be a scientist at the Medical College by day and a social worker at Hull House by night.

Living at Hull House was quite an experience for Alice. The other tenants were true leaders. Alice described herself as "a lonely, stranded heathen among many elect," but slowly she gained the respect of her peers and found friends, companionship, intellectual stimulation, and most importantly, the excitement of being involved in an important cause. Members of Hull House were required to dedicate some of their time to social activism. While conducting research at the College, Alice would also teach evening classes to people in the neighborhood, take the neighborhood children on outings, and devote Saturday mornings to bathing neighborhood babies, which eventually grew into Chicago's first baby health-care center.

The needs of the impoverished community in which Alice lived, however, were too great and her efforts appeared to have no real impact, causing her to feel she was hopelessly inadequate and that her scientific work was both "remote and useless." She wasn't merely visiting the slums of a city, she was living in one. Her neighbors lived under terrible conditions — crowded tenements, rats, pestilence, poverty, and disease. Alice yearned to help these people. She would talk with her neighbors frequently, learning about their poor nutrition, their long hours at the factories, and other poor working conditions. Many of her neighbors grew ill and Alice set out to find out why. At the time, people thought that these diseases were caused by exhaustion, but Alice could see alarming patterns. Like a detective, Alice investigated these patterns and started to believe that workers in certain jobs were contracting specific types of diseases. Were these diseases somehow related to the particular factory or industry?

By this time, Alice was thirty years old and one of America's leading experts on bacteria. She began her detective work with a passion. Since there were hardly any medical records kept, Alice found herself walking through Chicago's slums, entering the homes of factory workers and interviewing them. How was their health? What were they eating? Where did they work? Alice was the first person that ever seemed to care about the lives of these people, and everyone opened their doors to her and provided her with all of the information she wanted. Through hundreds of personal interviews, Alice slowly collected proof for her theory that certain illnesses were connected to certain industries.

Painters and people who worked in the lead factories were developing indigestion and occasionally had problems with their joints. Stock yard employees were developing pneumonia and rheumatism. Workers in steel mills confessed they were often exhausted. Alice began to suspect that theses diseases were caused by conditions in the factories themselves and were not simply a result of fatigue.

In 1902, the Northwestern's Women's Medical School closed and Alice found a position at the newly-founded Memorial Institute for Infectious Diseases as an assistant to the eminent pathologist, Dr. Ludwig Hektoen. Here, she received encouragement from the scientific community and began her scientific work with renewed vigor. That year typhoid fever hit Chicago. Alice again began working like a detective and investigated the cause of this disease. She then wrote a paper on typhoid fever and how flies were spreading this horrible disease. As a result of her published findings, the Chicago Health Department underwent a total reform.

Alice received much public acclaim for her efforts and quickly became recognized for being both a scientist and a leading member of Chicago's social reform circles. Her home, however, was still Hull House, and Alice was still determined to discover what was causing her neighbors and friends to grow ill and die. At the same time, Alice continued to sense that the work she had always longed to do had eluded her. Even after all the recognition she received and the change she had helped to bring about, and after ten years of living at Hull House, Alice felt that she would "never be more than a fourth-rate scientist."

Alice then came across a book that would change the course of her life, giving her the inspiration and courage to save thousands of lives and change the way America ran its industries and factories. The book was *The Dangerous Trades*, written by Sir Thomas Oliver. In this book, Oliver documented numerous health risks posed by various industries in England. Alice immediately tried to find any literature written about the conditions of American factories, but it was a lost cause since nothing had ever been written about the dangers of any particular trade in America.

Unlike countries in Europe, the United States had never paid attention to diseases that might be caused in the workplace. Furthermore, there were no occupational safety laws in America. There were also very few unions to protect the workers' rights and no medical records that documented the deaths and diseases of workers in factories and other new industries. Alice saw that the basic human rights of our nation's lower-class workers were being ignored. Finally, Alice knew exactly where to apply her energies. She discovered a way in which her knowledge of pathology could help the common person. Unfortunately, since there were no records or documentation of any kind, Alice had to create an entirely new field of study on her own.

In 1908, at the age of 39, Alice published an article emphasizing the need for better working conditions. Americans were now familiar with Alice's ideas and theories about the dangers of industry, but she had no proof to back up her theories. Alice continued to investigate diseases that might be caused by poor working conditions in factories by again going door to door in the slums interviewing people. Although workers feared losing their jobs, Alice's determination and genuine concern for their health and well-being encouraged them. She kept meticulous records of her findings in hopes of garnering scientific proof for her theories.

This same year, a man named John Andrews brought to Hull House the first bit of proof for which Alice had been searching. John Andrews studied the disease called "Phossy Jaw," an illness contracted by only one group of people — workers in match factories. In these factories, workers were breathing in fumes of the dangerous phosphorus used in making matches. Prolonged exposure to phosphorus caused the workers to develop phossy jaw. Most Americans did not believe that this disease existed in the United States but Mr. Andrew's findings proved without a doubt that the disease did in fact exist and it was caused by working in match factories. He found over 150 match workers who contracted phossy jaw. Two years later, a law was passed banning the use of phosphorus in match factories, which effectively eliminated phossy jaw in the United States. Slowly, America began to realize that many of its industries and trades were dangerous. The governor of Illinois asked Alice to head a select, nine-member panel whose sole purpose would be to investigate the hygiene of various factories and to catalogue all industries that were hazardous to the health of the workers.

Alice acted as the managing director of the Occupational Disease Commission for nine years, studying industrial poisons, toxic substances, and other contaminants. Alice personally visited hundreds of mills, mines, factories, and other industrial plants to collect the necessary scientific data to prove which were the dangerous trades and why. While on this committee, Alice specialized in the investigation of lead poisoning. She began her research by touring factories all around Illinois, interviewing workers whom she knew worked with lead. She would spend hours reading patient histories in hospitals, desperate to find clues. When she found people who had lead poisoning, she went to their homes to speak with them. Alice soon discovered that enamel workers had been developing the very same symptoms and sicknesses as the lead workers. She toured the enameling factories and found that the factories were flooded with thick clouds of enamel dust. Alice tested the enamel and found that twenty percent of the enamel was actually lead. This proved that enameling could give someone lead poisoning, and enameling was now documented as yet another dangerous trade. In 1911, at the age of 41, Alice and her committee submitted a report on the dangerous trades. Alice had personally discovered 77 trades that used lead and over 500 cases of lead poisoning within these trades. This report led Illinois to pass an occupational disease law in 1911. Finally, employers were required to follow safety precautions and provide monthly check-ups for workers who handled certain dangerous substances.

This was tremendous progress for both Alice and America. Researching the dangerous trades, however, was still a new area of study and if more progress was to be made, it would require national attention and resources. Alice made it her crusade to ensure that all of the dangerous trades were identified and that all workers were being protected in the workplace. The committee sent Alice to the International Congress on Occupational Accidents and Diseases in Brussels, in hopes that she could gain further insight into her investigations.

While in Brussels, Alice presented a paper on the conditions in America's industrial workplace. Considering that European nations had already spent a significant amount of time and resources investigating their dangerous trades, most people at the international conference found that the conditions in American factories were drastically below the standards already set by the world community. She was informed that it was well known that there was no industrial hygiene in America. Alice was not the only American citizen to be ashamed by this. The U.S. Commissioner of Labor also happened to be in Brussels to witness the embarrassment. Upon returning to the United States, Alice Hamilton was asked to conduct nationwide research on the dangerous trades. Due to Alice's painstaking research, the United States government was taking steps for the first time in its history to eliminate dangers in the workplace and to protect all of its citizens from inhumane working conditions.

Alice spent years traveling around the nation, entering factory after factory, finding deplorable working conditions. Poisons and noxious fumes abounded, and Alice researched and catalogued each one she could find. Her unrelenting investigation of the dangerous trades would eventually lead her to personally explore 800-foot-deep copper mines. Nothing would stop Alice from investigating a particular trade, no matter how dangerous it appeared.

Her research was ground-breaking and Alice received national recognition for her efforts. In 1919, Alice was the first woman ever appointed a professor at Harvard, where she specialized in industrial medicine at Harvard's Medical School. Even though Alice was a nationally-known figure, heralded for uncovering and changing the dangerous trades, and even though Harvard had selected her to be its first female professor, Alice was treated unjustly based on her gender. She was denied basic privileges of being a member of Harvard's faculty. Among other things, she was denied tickets to the Harvard football games and was banned from sitting on the platform with the rest of the professors at commencement. Originally, Harvard had asked Alice to research dangers in department stores, but Alice refused. She knew what types of industries needed her help. Eventually, Harvard gave Alice the job she wanted — teaching for six months and spending the rest of her time continuing her surveys for the federal government.

Through Alice's continued efforts, our nation began passing worker's compensation laws and hygienic standards for industries. Countless lives were spared due to Alice's determination. Alice also spent a large portion of her life protesting World Wars I and II and advocating mediation as an alternative to war. She also spent time researching the horrors experienced by victims of the wars and tried to help Americans understand the ramifications of a full-scale war, as it wasn't being fought on American soil. Ironically, Alice, who was both a pacifist and an advocate for human rights, was under FBI surveillance for much of her life. For some reason, she was considered potentially subversive. Perhaps it was because she thought that both the lives of Americans and Germans were worth saving. Perhaps it was because she instigated radical reform in the way our nation conducted its businesses. Perhaps it was because Alice Hamilton boldly entered the exclusively male world of politics and industry.

Before dying in 1969, Alice Hamilton had traveled the world investigating and reporting on many injustices. Her achievements were numerous: in 1924 she was the only woman member of the League of Nations Health Committee; she was invited by the Soviet Union's Department of Health to visit and inspect their facilities; she observed the effects of the Nazi Government in 1933, and again in 1938, as a delegate to the International Congress of Occupational Accidents and Diseases; she wrote an autobiography in 1943 entitled *Exploring the Dangerous Trades*; she was elected president of the National Consumer's League; she received Honorary degrees from Smith College, Mt. Holyoke College, University of Michigan, University of Rochester, and Tulane University; and she became a member of the American Association for the Advancement of Science and the American Public Health and Medical Associations.

Perhaps her greatest public recognition occurred in 1947, when she was the first woman to receive the Lasker Award of the U.S. Public Health Department. The Lasker award, the most prestigious in the field of public health, is presented to pioneers in the field of hygienic and industrial disease research and to those who develop methods for preventing occupational related ailments. It said of the recipient, "no one has achieved more in this field." Certainly Alice Hamilton, more so than anyone else in her day, was the most deserving of this award.

Chapter 5

ະ⊃ଔ

Florence Rena Sabin

Central City, Colorado was one of the many western United States mining towns that attracted seekers of great fortune in the late nineteenth century. People raised in the more densely populated states of the East Coast often traveled across America in search of land and precious minerals, and for the fulfillment of America's promise of opportunity for all. In this environment, a young girl came of age who would one day be considered one of the most eminent of living women scientists. Though her family had a history of intellectual and progressive women, Florence Rena Sabin never imagined that she had the power to unlock great anatomical secrets, or that her accomplishments would make such a deep impression on the world that she would be immortalized in the annals of science.

Florence's family had a history of traveling great distances to achieve their goals and of making every effort to develop their intellectual talents and skills. Her father, George Kimball Sabin, was the son of a New England country doctor and had himself studied medicine for two years. But in search of his own destiny, he struck out for Colorado to take advantage of the mining opportunities in the West.

Florence's mother, Rena Sabin, was infused with a fiery and adventurous spirit. Born and educated in Vermont, she traveled to the

Source: Colorado Historical Society

South in the 1850s to teach. When the Civil War broke out and prospects of teaching in that region became non-existent or dangerous, she received a special permit from General Sherman to continue her teaching in the West. There she settled in Central City, Colorado and met the fortune-seeking George Sabin. They fell in love, married, and in 1869 bore their first child, Florence's sister, Mary. On November 9, 1871, Florence was born.

The Sabin sisters received similar educational opportunities. Their primary schooling was in Denver and final preparation for college was at schools in Vermont. Both sisters were destined for Smith College. Mary, being the older sister, graduated first and was offered an assistantship in Astronomy. But Mary was more interested in promoting Florence's education and turned the offer down. She returned to Denver to teach mathematics at East High School and help her family fund Florence's tuition.

What motivated Mary's actions is unclear because although Florence had proven herself a capable student, she did not stand out in any way. She made good grades, met all the challenges set before her, and had achieved a good class standing, but had given no indication of the great scientific mind that would guide the world to new levels of understanding and vision. She was, until her junior year at Smith, an average student without much focus on her future.

Then, in her third year, she happened to take a zoology class that opened up a side of Florence that she never suspected existed. Working the long laboratory hours required for the class, Florence noticed a change in herself. For the first time in her life, she became passionate about an academic pursuit. Social distractions no longer enticed her, and she began to spend most of her free time in the lab running experiments, not knowing where they would take her, but sure that the journey would be exciting. By the end of the course, she had found her calling — she would continue working in science and become a doctor.

It was a bold decision for Florence to make. At the time, the American public was accepting of women as doctors, but the medical schools in America were not. Separate medical schools for women had sprung up to meet the demand, but the more prestigious schools ignored them. In addition, the quality of America's medical programs were far below those of Europe. So, a woman seeking to become a medical doctor in America could only choose from second-rate schools in an already inferior pool. To Florence's great fortune, however, history had a surprise in store for her.

Johns Hopkins University was, at that time, just breaking ground on what would become one of the most prestigious medical colleges in America. The goal of the University was to establish a medical school that equaled or surpassed the quality of European medical schools. But soon the University ran into financial difficulties. Unable to continue funding the new school on its own, the University was obliged to look elsewhere for philanthropic funding. A coterie of wealthy Baltimore women came to the rescue. Small in number, but armed with overflowing coffers, the women made their funding contingent on two provisions for the medical college: 1) that women be admitted on equal criteria with men; and 2) that the overall requirements for entrance be made much more stringent than Johns Hopkins had originally planned. The Board was strongly opposed to these provisions, and was generally disgruntled at being ordered about by a group of female socialites. The Board tried desperately to secure funds elsewhere, but the search proved fruitless, and the University was faced with the prospect of the financial failure of their medical school plans. It agreed to the women's demands just in time for Florence to begin the next phase of her great journey.

After graduating from Smith College with a Bachelor of Science degree in 1893, Florence taught for three years. Then, in 1896, she entered the new medical school at Johns Hopkins University. At Johns Hopkins, Florence immediately blossomed. Some of the greatest medical professors had been lured to the new school, and under the tutelage of these great teachers, Florence quickly set herself apart from her other classmates. She demonstrated her natural abilities at accurate and original observation in the laboratory. These particular abilities would be the powers by which she would distinguish herself in history.

Working under the anatomist Dr. Franklin P. Mall, Florence began a piece of original research that would become the envy of her peers. She was studying the anatomy of the brain, and decided to construct a model of the brain stem of a new born child. Her model was so accurate and so complete that it was reproduced by a German model-making firm and soon found its way into medical schools all over the world. Although a small accomplishment by the later standards of her scientific career, this moment symbolized the special gift that Florence had to offer the world – the ability to see and uncover the secrets of science and, simultaneously, the ability to reveal to the world what she saw.

Florence received her medical degree from Johns Hopkins in 1900. In addition to the brain stem model she had created, Florence's study of brain anatomy also yielded her first book, *An Atlas of the Medulla and Mid-Brain,* published in 1901, just a year after she received her degree.

Florence had distinguished herself so prominently during her medical training that she was offered a rare opportunity for a young female doctor of the day — an internship at the Johns Hopkins Hospital. At the hospital, Florence discovered that she preferred research to practicing medicine. She longed to be in the laboratory teasing out mysteries and gaining new knowledge, rather than treating patients with what was already known. But unfortunately almost all research laboratories were closed to women. Then, as Florence's first year out of graduate school came to a close, another group of wealthy Baltimore women indirectly entered her life and, like unknown guardian angels, opened up to Florence the closed path she so desperately wanted to follow.

The Baltimore Association for the Advancement of University Education of Women established a fellowship at Johns Hopkins medical school that would give women graduates the opportunity to continue real, in-depth scientific research along with their male counterparts. Florence was awarded the fellowship in 1902 and returned to the medical school as an assistant in the Anatomy Department, working under Dr. Mall, an anatomy professor who had inspired a younger Florence to the levels of excellence that had begun to mark every step of her life.

Working with Dr. Mall, Florence developed a research project that, entirely unknown to the curious young scientist, was destined to bring her to the forefront of modern medical science, as well as focus much-deserved attention on the fledgling Johns Hopkins Medical School both for its level of excellence and the vital role of the women students and doctors in establishing and maintaining that excellence. Florence was to undertake a study of a little understood and medically controversial subject — the origin and development of the lymphatic system.

Working under Dr. Mall's advice, encouragement, and sometimes intellectual opposition, Florence delved into her mysterious subject with great tenacity. She obtained pig embryos, at varying stages of development, from a local slaughterhouse to use as the base of her study. Her early work with these embryos led her to postulate a possible mode and origin for the development of the lymphatic system. For this initial work on her subject, Florence garnered her first major science award, the Naples Table Association Prize for 1903, which carried a $1,000 cash prize and was offered for original scientific thesis work by a woman. In addition, this initial work inspired other scientists around the world to begin their own research into the lymphatic system. Florence continued her research as well. Although she proceeded with great care and commitment, Florence's work was not without its detractors. Florence nonetheless forged ahead without much concern for such distractions and was eventually able to demonstrate that lymphatic vessels develop from a special layer of cells in certain fetal veins, rather than, as had previously been held, from intercellular spaces. She also demonstrated that the lymphatic vessels emerged from these venous "buds" and developed outward as channels that branched and bathed all the body's cells. These discoveries would become the first of many milestones for Dr. Sabin. In her career as a medical researcher, this was simply her first great step.

The fellowship that carried her through her lymphatic system research expired in 1905, but she had so distinguished herself and Johns Hopkins Medical School with her work that she was appointed to the faculty of the School as an Associate Professor of Anatomy. Florence's career was moving along quite nicely; she had established herself as a research scientist of the highest caliber at what was becoming one of the world's best medical colleges.

As an associate professor, Dr. Sabin also distinguished herself among the teaching staff. Although most of her students were male, and had come from male-exclusive undergraduate programs, none of her students seemed to have anything other than great respect for her. The dean of Johns Hopkins Medical School remarked in 1911 that one of the most successful teachers on the faculty was a woman. Her secret was that she did not teach her students through the method that the great educational theorist, Paolo Friere, called the "banking method of education." Rather than treating her students as empty vessels into which she would "deposit" knowledge in "infallible" chunks, she taught her students to discover for themselves. She led them to knowledge, but they, themselves would perceive and possess it. Her method of teaching was that of personal discovery and original thought. Because of this and her research, she was instrumental both as a student and as a faculty member in raising Johns Hopkins to a place of pre-eminence in the world of medical academia. For these accomplishments, Dr. Sabin was rewarded with another first. In 1917, she was made Professor of Histology (the study of microscopic anatomy), becoming the first woman to receive the rank of full professor at Johns Hopkins Medical School. Unfortunately, for several decades she was the only woman to receive this honor.

She continued her research and teaching at Johns Hopkins until 1925. During that time she distinguished herself in several ways. Recognized as one of the great women scientists in America, Dr. Sabin was invited to speak at the public reception honoring Madame Curie at Carnegie Hall in 1921. But this recognition was soon to be overshadowed. Building on techniques she developed during her research into the lymphatic system, Dr. Sabin turned her attentions to the origin of blood vessels. In this research, however, she wanted to expand her scientific vision. Not content with studying a series of dead embryos like time-lapse photographs of biological development, Dr. Sabin looked for a method to study live embryos. She used a method of hanging drop preparations to observe the development of chick embryos. Her work paid off as she became the first person to witness the birth of blood vessels in a living organism and was able, through this research, to demonstrate that the red corpuscles develop from the endothelial cells of the veins.

This research, the second great stage of her scientific career, brought her three more milestones. In 1924, Dr. Sabin was the first woman elected president of the American Association of Anatomists. In 1925, she became the first woman elected to the National Academy of Sciences. The same year, she was also offered a membership at the Rockefeller Institute for Medical Research (now Rockefeller University), becoming the first woman to be offered a membership at the prestigious institute.

Her focus at the Institute was researching tuberculosis, the great plague raging through America. Although Dr. Sabin worked for thirteen years with a team of astute assistants and scientists, the tuberculosis research would ultimately prove unsuccessful. The team did manage, however, to provide other researchers with significant evidence and knowledge from which to proceed, especially on the role of monocytes in forming tubercles. But, in 1938, at the age of 57, Florence retired from medical research at the Rockefeller Institute and returned to Denver and her family.

During her years at the Rockefeller Institute, Florence had obtained several more honors. She was awarded the Annual Achievement Award by *Pictorial Review* in 1928, the National Achievement Award in 1932, and the M. Carey Thomas Prize in Science in 1935, which was given to her at the celebration marking the fiftieth anniversary of the founding of Bryn Mawr College. In 1934, she published a biography of her mentor at Johns Hopkins entitled, *Franklin Paine Mall: The Story of a Mind.* Florence Sabin had a career of which any research scientist would be proud. But Dr. Sabin was not yet done. After eight years of retirement, she was called to task once more.

In 1944, the Governor of Colorado, John Vivian, was developing a committee to look into possible solutions for common public health problems. As an esteemed scientist in histology, and with her long history of studying tuberculosis, Dr. Sabin was an excellent candidate to spearhead the campaign. She developed and lobbied for a reorganization of the state health system, which included stricter controls of infectious disease, contaminated milk, and sewage disposal. Her efforts proved successful when the Colorado legislature passed the "Sabin Health Laws" in 1946, incorporating her suggestions and plans into the public health system. She was subsequently appointed chairman of the Interim Board of Health and Hospitals of Denver, and the Manager of Health and Charities for Denver, the salary from which she donated completely to medical research. She served in these civil posts until 1953 when she resumed her retirement. On October 3 of that year, Dr. Florence Rena Sabin died quietly in her home.

As with many of the scientists in this book, it is hard to grasp the exact nature of Dr. Sabin's contributions to the world of science. She cured no disease and she invented no great contraption. What she did do, however, was to teach others to see what they had been unable to see. She revealed how the smallest and yet most significant vessels of the body, the lymphatic and blood vessels, originated and developed. She demonstrated how a woman could rise through the ranks of the male-dominated field of science and academia. Through her career and life, Dr. Sabin showed that destiny is what you make of it, and when you look closely enough, and long enough at your subject, great mysteries may unfold.

Chapter 6

೫)ೞ

Lillian Moller Gilbreth

On June 17, 1924, three days after her husband Frank unexpectedly died, Dr. Lillian Moller Gilbreth stood in front of her fourteen-room farmhouse in Montclair, New Jersey to bid good-bye to her eleven children. She was on her way to Europe to take over Frank's speaking engagements on motion study, an industrial engineering technique pioneered by the couple. She would be giving lectures and guidance to members of both the London Power Conference in England and the World Congress of Scientific Management in Czechoslovakia. This was one of the most important journeys she would take in her life. If she was successfully received, she would be able to keep both her career and her enormous family intact; if not, she would be forced to move herself and her children into her parents' home in California, and her career as the first female industrial consulting engineer would be over.

Lillian Moller was born on May 24, 1878 in Oakland, California, the oldest of eight children. Her parents, William and Annie Moller, were both from wealthy families. Her father's family ran a prosperous sugar refinery in New York and her mother's family developed real estate in Oakland. After they were married, the Mollers made Oakland their home and William became a partner in a thriving retail hardware

Source: Rutgers University Archives/Special Collections

business. The combined prestige of her parents' backgrounds and her father's successful partnership made the Moller family one of the most respected families in their community.

Dr. Gilbreth's upbringing was, like her adult life, a struggle between two extremes: home and study. Her mother was often ill and often pregnant. As the oldest child and a girl, Lillian was required to oversee her mother's sickbed and, as younger siblings were born, to oversee the care of her brothers and sisters. These domestic roles, forced on Lillian at such a young age, would never be roles she was comfortable with. She preferred more intellectual pursuits.

To her great fortune, Lillian's parents were supportive of her personal and intellectual development. She received private tutoring from her mother until age nine. At that point, she entered the Oakland public school system. When she was a teenager, her parents allowed her to study music with composer, John Metcalfe. She wrote the verses for his song "Sunrise." The Mollers also thought their daughter should see more of the country than just Oakland, and by the time she graduated from high school, she had traveled across America three times.

Although Lillian accepted the enormous responsibility of her role as the oldest daughter with grace, the childhood experiences she would later consider most formative were her experiences studying poetry and music. She would even continue her musical studies into her adulthood because she did not want to lose these special skills. This perseverance would ultimately allow Lillian Moller to become Dr. Lillian Gilbreth, the world's first female consulting engineer and the re-inventor of the American workspace.

Before she could make her mark on the world, however, Lillian needed to attain a higher education. Although her parents had been supportive of her elementary and high school academic pursuits, they were at first opposed to her desire to attend the University of California at Berkeley. There was no question that Lillian could be a successful and productive college student, but it was the end of the nineteenth century, and American society was not yet convinced that intellectual pursuits were proper for a woman. After much consideration and discussion, however, her parents relented and she enrolled at Berkeley.

At college, Lillian studied literature. She received a bachelor's degree in 1900 and the University chose her as its first female commencement day speaker. Lillian was on a roll now, and decided to continue her academic studies. She moved to Manhattan and enrolled at Columbia University to continue her studies in English literature. She found New

York City unpleasant, however, and returned to Berkeley to complete her studies. She wrote a thesis on Ben Jonson's *Bartholomew Fair*, and received a master's degree in English in 1902. She pushed onward with her scholarly pursuits by enrolling in a doctorate program in psychology the following year, again at the University of California. That spring, however, Lillian took a fateful trip.

From childhood, Lillian had been a rather quiet and unassuming person, preferring to be alone to enjoy the private pursuits of a scholar. She did not seek fame or glory. Her ambitions were more intellectual, and to achieve them, she always tried to maintain a discreet and "uneventful" life. Drawing on the strength that had helped her achieve her goals, she was always able to deal with the unexpected interruptions of life. She had decided to take a much needed break from her academic career. With the help of her parents, Lillian had arranged to be part of a chaperoned trip, with several other wealthy Oakland daughters, to Europe. During the first leg of this journey, while spending some time in Boston, she encountered the person that would irrevocably alter the path of her life: Frank Gilbreth.

Frank Gilbreth was born in 1868 in Fairfield, Maine. His father died when Frank was three years old, leaving Frank to be raised by his mother. She instilled in Frank and his two older sisters the belief that they were born to change the world, and to that end she tried to focus her children on education. However, Frank, as would always be so, preferred the experiential to the abstract and, after graduating from high school, he took a job as a bricklayer to work his way up the ladder of construction engineering. It was at this job that Frank first began to formulate the idea of "motion study." He observed the various ways that different bricklayers went about their work and, based on these observations, began to suggest standardized methods that would ensure the most efficient laying of brick. He also invented a scaffold that would keep loose bricks at the top level of the wall being built. The foremen and contractors he worked with were so impressed with Frank's work that he quickly rose through the ranks and, by the age of twenty-seven he was a wealthy consulting engineer who operated out of offices in New York, Boston, and London.

Lillian's chaperone to Europe, Frank's cousin, introduced Frank to the entourage of young ladies. His eyes fell on Lillian. He convinced her to go for a ride in his "horseless carriage" and they took a wild, bumpy, dusty whirl through the streets of Boston. On this drive Lillian first became exposed to and enamored of Frank's personality: boisterous, jocular, slightly vulgar, and easily riled. This was quite the opposite of Lillian's more genteel and scholarly air. After she left Europe, Frank went to California to court her.

Lillian and Frank were married on October 19, 1904 at the Moller home in Oakland. Their wedding announcement in the local paper referred to Lillian's academic accomplishments as a two-time college graduate and member of Phi Beta Kappa, stating: "Although a graduate of the University of California, the bride is nonetheless an extremely attractive young woman." This idea that Lillian's successes were "in spite of" her "finer female qualities," and that she was pursuing goals not appropriate to her gender, would always haunt her as she quietly struggled for acceptance as a woman of great intelligence.

On the honeymoon train departing California, Lillian and Frank had a discussion that would come to typify both their personal relationship and their work relationship. The subject was children. The discussion was conducted like a business meeting — various options were being put on the table and considered in an orderly fashion. They mutually decided that they should have a large family and the number of children was set at "an even dozen." Even the preferred sex of the children was decided — six boys and six girls. *Cheaper by the Dozen*, a biography of the family written by two of the Gilbreth children, Frank Jr. and Ernestine, describes that when the discussion was concluded, Frank took out his memorandum book and solemnly wrote: "Don't forget to have six boys and six girls." Such would be the Gilbreth lifestyle: planning and efficiency was not just for the workplace — they were concepts by which every area of life would be guided. The person who had a plan and followed it through efficiently, the Gilbreth's believed, would ensure themselves happiness and success. As Lillian would discover, such theories, so clean and simple on paper, become messy and complex in the real world.

The Gilbreths moved to New York where Frank headquartered his construction engineering business. Though they immediately began to follow through on their plan for twelve children, neither Lillian nor her husband expected Lillian to become exclusively a homemaker, which, by her own accounts and the accounts of her children, she was never very good at anyway. Instead, she spent her time working in partnership with Frank on the expanding business of motion study. It was a partnership so fruitful that it would come to change both the management and physical processes of a world wide industry.

Working together, Frank and Lillian complimented each other. As they explored and refined motion study, Frank, with his physical and mechanical experience in industry, focused mostly on process: What was the task? What tools were available? What tools could be brought in or constructed to facilitate and speed up the task? Lillian, with her background in psychology and the humanities, focused mostly on what would come to be known as the "psychology of management." Rather than approaching an engineering question as purely mechanical, Lillian approached it as a human question: How may a task be better executed so that the worker experiences less fatigue, avoids injury, and, consequently, is more productive? This component transformed Frank's solid efficiency ideas into some of the greatest industrial management theories of the twentieth century.

During the first few years of their marriage, Lillian worked mostly at home. Her primary work, besides having children, was as editor of Frank's numerous publications in engineering and industry journals. Later, after Frank closed his construction engineering business in New York and moved the family to Providence, Rhode Island, Lillian entered Brown University to complete her psychology doctorate, which she had discontinued when she married Frank. In 1914, she published a book based on the work she and her husband were doing, titled *Psychology of Management*. The following year, Brown awarded her a Ph.D. in psychology. From that point on, she would become an integral part of her husband's business. No longer just a silent partner, she began to tour with Frank to engineering lectures, seminars, and job sites where they worked side by side to help industries and factories discover what Frank called "the one best way" to organize a workforce and workspaces. But Lillian still insisted that she be introduced as Mrs. Frank Gilbreth when they made business appearances. This self-effacement proved to be one of her greatest obstacles, and it would ultimately almost destroy her career.

When the Gilbreths were discussing their twelve-children plan, Lillian asked her husband: "How on earth could anybody raise twelve children and continue a career?" Frank said: "We teach management, so we shall have to practice it." One of the Gilbreths' beliefs was that efficiency was independent of environment – that is, the methods used to make a factory more productive and harmonious could also be used to make the home and home-life more productive and harmonious. They themselves utilized this theory.

Their home became a laboratory for ideas and methods of efficiency, and they organized the raising of their children in the way they believed management should organize its workers. The children were required to record on progress charts various pieces of information as they grew: height, weight, chores, hygiene practices, etc. There was also a strict set of rules about how the household would be run and what each child's role in that system would be. To facilitate this plan, the Gilbreths established in their home an entity which they also promoted in the workplace: a council composed of both management (parents) and workers (children).

This family council, at which all members were given equal right to motion, argue, and vote, would become the primary way the Gilbreth family made its decisions, and it would be used until Lillian's death. These methods also became, unintentionally, Lillian's first experiments in a field with which she would come to be identified independently of her husband: home engineering. She shared these ideas with the world through independent articles such as "Running a Home for Eleven Kids," which appeared in *Collier's* magazine on July 21, 1923.

The Gilbreths also kept an office in a separate room of their house, and from this office they ran their consulting firm, Gilbreth Inc. (in which Lillian was a full partner with Frank). They would tour the factories of their clients, which included Eastman Kodak and Remington Typewriter, and collect on-site data. The most important data they collected were motion pictures of workers performing their jobs. They would then review the films at home, and by discrete and scientific analysis of the task and the worker's movements, they would determine the most efficient method for the worker to follow, often prescribing the redesign of a workspace to eliminate what the Gilbreth's considered the greatest waste of all, physical exertion. They also held lectures and demonstrations at their in-home office for managers and engineers, demonstrating how they could use the same analytical methods to better run and design their businesses.

By the 1920s, the Gilbreths were two of the most successful and noted American engineers, and the field they had pioneered, motion study, had become an integral part of engineering methodology. As a result, the Gilbreths had more clients than they could handle.

It looked like the Gilbreths' lives were running according to plan, but that was not to be when, in 1924, Frank died. He was on his way to deliver lectures at two engineering conferences in Europe. He called

Lillian from the train station in Montclair, New Jersey, where the family had moved after Lillian received her doctorate. He had had a motion saving idea for one of their clients that he wanted to share with Lillian. Before he could speak more than ten words to her, he collapsed from a heart attack. Lillian heard her life crumble in the silence of the phone line.

From that point on, Lillian could no longer live the quiet, self-effacing life she had grown used to. Without her husband to head Gilbreth, Inc., she would have to show her own face to the world. The family, although well-off, was not independently wealthy. Most of their money had gone to raising their enormous family, all of whom they believed should get college educations. The rest of their income had been reinvested in the business. Without a viable income, the Gilbreth clan would be forced to split apart and live with various relatives. Lillian would have to take over Gilbreth, Inc. completely to save both her career and her family. Her first order of business was to fulfill Frank's speaking obligations in London and Czechoslovakia. Her future success, she believed, rested heavily on these engagements. She left for Europe only three days after her husband's death, choosing perseverance over mourning.

The world did not receive her well. Although her lectures in Europe went without complications, and although she had been the first woman accepted as a member of the Society of Industrial Engineers in 1921 (honorary, and by virtue of her partnership with Frank), the owners and managers of world industry did not grant her the respect she worked for and deserved. Long-time clients of Gilbreth, Inc. canceled their contracts. The reasons given were all similar: they did not believe a woman could successfully perform the work of an engineer alone, and they did not think Lillian could command the cooperation of factory foremen and floor workers, an important component of motion study. None of these setbacks, however, would keep Lillian from achieving her goals and maintaining her place in the world.

Lillian assessed the situation and came to two conclusions. First, for an immediate financial solution, she looked more closely at the idea of teaching motion study to others. If industry did not think she could perform the practical duties of motion study, they at least acknowledged she was the world's foremost living expert of the theory. She designed a "Motion Study School," which she intended to run out of her home. She sent out proposals to several former clients and received eight students in return.

Lillian's second conclusion was that, if industry did not think she could be of use in the male-dominated world of big factories, perhaps it would be more accepting if she put her engineering expertise to use in fields associated more commonly with women. She began to formulate ideas and devices that would use motion study to bring efficiency management to the place where most women of the 1920s spent their time — in the home. Her first big success was the idea of the "efficiency kitchen." With the help of her students, Lillian created blueprints for an electric food mixer, new designs for stoves and refrigerators, and a centralized groundplan for the "modern" kitchen, which included her original idea of a "circular workspace." A later addition to this home workspace was assessing the optimal counter height, so that women would experience less fatigue from bending to reach counter tops.

Ironically, Lillian herself never had a modern kitchen. She was not, after all, a homemaker in the traditional sense. She was only responding to others' needs. If, as a woman, the world would only respect her ideas if those ideas related to "women's work," then that was where she would apply her engineering talents. She would make herself, at least on paper, into an expert homemaker. This ruse worked. Media flocked to her door, unable to resist the story of a woman engineer with eleven kids redesigning the American kitchen based on scientific principles. Based on this work she received her first solo contract from a New York-based electric appliance manufacturing company.

Lillian accomplished all of this within the first year after Frank's death. It was probably the most difficult year of her life. In *Cheaper by the Dozen*, her children describe her as being physically fatigued, sleeping only a few hours a day as she worked endlessly so that neither her family nor her career would suffer. In the end, her efforts would win her the respect and prestige so long denied her.

By the end of the 1920s, Lillian's reputation as an efficiency engineer far surpassed any fame she and her husband had achieved together. Motion study became a common tool in the development of mass-production, the most important industrial concept of that decade. And Lillian's media-hyped expertise in this field worked to her great advantage. By the 1930s, many of Gilbreth, Inc.'s former clients sought contracts with Lillian and she was once again on top in her field.

For the remainder of her life, Lillian was able to harvest the fruits of her labor. She continued as a consulting engineer and lecturer well into her seventies. She continued to pioneer management theories that empowered workers and relieved them from both physical and psychological fatigue, such as the employee suggestion box and the more general idea of employee participation in management decisions. During World War II, the American government hired her to apply motion study to the War Manpower Commission and to help develop rehabilitation programs for disabled veterans. She worked for Purdue University as a professor of management and a consultant on careers for women. Colleagues at Purdue would credit her with creating a more realistic attitude among the faculty and students toward the human factor in management and also the place of women in industry. She received more than a dozen honorary degrees in her lifetime and, in 1966, she was the first woman to be awarded the Hoover Medal for distinguished public service by an engineer.

Through quiet but diligent effort, and armed with the belief that she could accomplish any task she set her mind to, Dr. Lillian Moller Gilbreth became one of the most respected engineers in the world, and the first well-known female engineer. Leaving the world more efficient and industry and management more humane than when she had found them, Dr. Lillian Gilbreth died of a stroke on January 2, 1972 in Scotsdale, Arizona. She was 93 years old.

Chapter 7

ೕಚಀ

Lise Meitner

L ise Meitner quietly entered the basement laboratory through a private entrance. No women were allowed upstairs in 1907. It was in this damp cellar that she initiated one of the greatest experiments of the century — the splitting of the atom. She did not stay in the basement for long.

Lise Meitner was born into a Viennese family in 1878 as the third of eight children. Her father, Phillip Meitner, was raised by Jewish parents but claimed to be agnostic. A lawyer with an inquisitive mind, he urged his children to learn about the wonders of science. Lise's mother, Hedwig Skovran Meitner, was a talented pianist who encouraged the children to appreciate the beauty of music. From them, Lise developed a passion for both music and physics. Lise would later write: "I am filled with deep gratitude for the unusual goodness of my parents, and the extraordinarily stimulating intellectual atmosphere in which my sisters and brothers and I grew up."

By the time Lise was a teenager, it was obvious that she was vastly different from the other children at the School for Elevated Daughters. Although she yearned for a formal higher education, the Viennese education system extended only to the ninth grade for girls. At the time, the majority believed that girls at age fourteen had learned enough to

Source: AIP Emilio Segrè Visual Archives, Herzfeld Collection

please a husband, raise children, and run a household. But Lise Meitner had no interest in marriage or running a household — she wanted to study physics.

The president of the National Bureau of Standards in Germany had recently announced: "Nothing else has to be done in physics than just make better measurements." Although discouraged by her family and a society in which physics was considered an empty, dead-end field (even for men), she was determined. Her father was worried that Lise would not be able to support herself practicing physics and insisted that she spend three years earning a certificate to teach French in girls' finishing schools. If she did, he promised to hire a private tutor to assist with the university entrance exam preparations. She reluctantly followed her father's advice.

At the age of 21, Lise held her father to his promise and began studying with a private tutor. She studied diligently, eager to pass the university entrance exams. Whenever she took a break, her younger brothers and sisters teased her: "Lise, you're going to flunk. You have just walked through the room without studying!" Due to her own fervor, discipline, and a talented, stimulating tutor named Arthur Szawasy, Lise completed eight years of school work, including eight years of Latin and six years of Greek, in just two years. Lise was one of four students to pass the university exam in 1901, just after Austria had opened its university doors to women. She enrolled at the University of Vienna for the following semester.

Meitner confessed that during her first year at the university, she attended too many lectures. In addition to her rigorous schedule, she attended daily lectures on subjects outside her field, such as history, politics, and literature. She was called a "fink," a name given to students who were not registered for a certain class but would "perch" themselves in the back of the lecture hall. Meitner was the only female fink.

As one of a handful of female students surrounded by hundreds of male students, university life was intimidating for Lise. There was an air of intolerance at the university. Although Lise was considered an oddity by most of society for her involvement in the predominately male world of academia, her music and an enthusiastic physics theory professor, Ludwig Boltzman, bolstered her spirits and kept her mind focused. Boltzman was considered an innovator in thermodynamics, and he gave Lise the vision of physics as "a battle for ultimate truth" — a vision she never lost. In 1905, Lise Meitner finished her dissertation on nonhomogeneous materials, becoming the second woman ever to earn a physics doctorate in Vienna.

Concerned about financial security, Lise dedicated the next year to teaching at a girls' high school. She could be found hidden deep in the library stacks of the university during her spare time. She became fascinated by the Curies' 1898 discovery of radium and savored newspaper accounts of the famous couple. She wanted to emulate the life of Marie Curie.

Meitner launched herself into a number of postdoctoral projects dealing with radium. Her first project involved a unique method to illustrate that alpha particles, emanating from naturally radioactive materials, are deflected slightly while traveling through matter. She used a piece of radium for the experiment, a piece donated by the Curies in thanks for Austria-Hungary's gift of pitchblende.

Eager to further her study abroad, Lise first contacted Marie Curie. Marie Curie rejected her because there was no position available at the Radium Institute; but her second choice, Max Planck, agreed to allow her to study at the University of Berlin. Although women were only allowed to audit classes in Prussian universities, Germany was considered the scientific center of the world at the time. In fact, its educated workforce was Germany's only natural resource. She left home at the age of 29, with a small allowance in her pocket and the anticipation of staying in Berlin maybe three or four semesters. She stayed in Berlin for 31 years.

Upon her arrival she introduced herself to Max Planck, who promptly asked Lise, "But you're a doctor already! What more do you want?" She wanted to gain a real and full understanding of physics. Despite Planck's unfavorable opinion of women in academia, Lise admired his quantum theory — that an atom absorbs and emits energy in specific units called quanta. She also admired his "rare honesty of mind" and "almost naive straightforwardness."

At this time Otto Hahn, a young German chemist who had worked with Earnest Rutherford on radioactivity, was looking for a collaborator. Hahn worked for professor Emil Fischer's chemistry institute which did not allow women in the building. With Rutherford's help, Fischer allowed Meitner to join Hahn in research, but she had to remain in the basement — a converted carpenter's shop.

It was a frustrating time for Meitner, not only because she was relegated to the bowels of the chemistry institute, but also because she could not learn through observation of her colleagues' experiments.

Despite the obvious problems, Hahn and Meitner published nine papers during the next two years. When Prussia declared that women could take courses for credit at the university, Fischer allowed Lise to work on the main floor of the institute. Prejudice, however, prevailed. For example, when Lise submitted an article to an encyclopedia editor, he liked it so much he asked if "Herr Meitner" would submit more. When he found the "Herr" was actually a "Fraulein," he wrote back stating that he would never dream of publishing anything written by a woman.

Hahn and Meitner were opposites, but they made a good team. Hahn was a foot taller than his five foot collaborator. He was outgoing and jovial, while she was shy and reserved. Hahn was intuitive in the laboratory, acting on instinct; Meitner deduced things logically and systematically. He was interested in new elements, while Meitner was more interested in understanding elements' radiation. During the countless hours of preparing chemically purified substances and monotonous calculations, the two often sang German folk songs together to pass the time.

Otto Hahn helped Lise get through years of gender discrimination. He insisted that she receive full credit for all of their work. He was her biggest supporter. Yet the two scientists, working night and day together, were never romantically linked, although both Meitner and Hahn acknowledged that they were very close friends. Meitner claimed she didn't have the time for romance. Many also believed Lise simply wasn't Hahn's type. Hahn claimed that Meitner had a strict ladylike upbringing and was very reserved, even shy.

Additionally, in Germany at the time, if a woman teacher or researcher was to marry she had to give up her professional life; and that Lise Meitner would never do. But with her large capacity for friendship, Lise never claimed that not marrying was an emotional sacrifice. She was satisfied with having male friends and colleagues, whose companionship was emotionally and intellectually satisfying. Those friends and colleagues included the world's greatest scientists: Albert Einstein, Max Planck, Niels Bohr, and Max Von Laue.

When scientific research institutes were established under the name of Kaiser Wilhelm, Emil Fischer managed to move Hahn and Meitner to the radiochemistry department of the new institute in 1912. That same year, Max Planck offered Meitner an assistantship. Although the stipend was small, it was better than being an unpaid guest researcher in Berlin. She thus became the first woman research assistant in Prussia. Although the position came with much prestige, it was inevitably coupled with much prejudice against her.

During World War I, Lise volunteered as an X-ray technician at a field hospital near the Austro-Italian border. She fainted on her first day. She longed for access to the laboratory and the comfort of peace. During this time she communicated with Hahn, who was already involved with poison-gas research. The two scientists found a rare radioactive element in pitchblende. The discovery earned her a position as head of the Radiophysics Department at the institute.

Barbara Jaeckel, a physicist who worked with Meitner recalled that, as the director of the institute, Meitner "was a distant boss. There was a wall between her and her underlings." Meitner was not of the garden variety. Although she was quite reserved, she controlled the institute with a firm hand. Wolfgang Paul, a 1989 Nobel Prize winner from the University of Bonn, remembered Meitner as a highly esteemed and strong woman who ruled the institute. Her nephew, Otto Frisch, teasingly called her "short, dark, and bossy." Meitner insisted that all personnel in contact with radium use toilet paper to open doors to avoid radioactive contamination. She even had those working with strong radiation sit in different chairs than those who worked with weaker elements. She was able to keep the first floor contamination-free for 25 years. With the financial backing of the I. G. Farben Corporation, Meitner's institute became comparable to the Curie Institute of Radium and Rutherford's Cavendish Laboratory in Cambridge — the premiere physics centers in the world.

The relationship between Hahn and Meitner took on a different tone during these years. They separated their laboratory team shortly after World War I as the study of Proactinium required the expertise of a physicist and a chemist. The once shy Meitner, who at one time addressed Otto Hahn as "Herr Hahn," now referred to him as "Hahnchen," the diminutive of Hahn. It was clear to the scientific world that she had pulled far ahead of Hahn professionally. Other physicists recognized that Lise was more famous than Hahn and that the glory of the Berlin Institute in the 1920s came mainly from Meitner. Indeed, she, and not Hahn, was among the people discussed for a Nobel Prize every year.

After the war, the first republican government was established in Germany. The Weimar Republic advanced the position of women in academics. It was only in 1922 that Meitner was allowed to lecture at the Berlin University. Her first lecture was entitled "Problems of Cosmic

Physics." The newspapers did little to capture the spirit of the talk by reporting on Meitner's "Cosmetic" Physics. Not until four years later did Meitner become Germany's first female physics professor.

Meitner was at the forefront of nuclear physics. Of particular interest to Meitner was how an electron, emitted by naturally radioactive substances, can be ejected by a radioactive nucleus with so much energy that the electron could not have existed within the nucleus originally. In 1934, Meitner took this on as the greatest and most complex experiment of the time. Irene Joliet-Curie, Enric Fermi, and Earnest Rutherford were also racing to solve the puzzle of the atom.

After much hesitation, Hahn agreed to team up with Meitner again in 1934 to assist with identifying new heavy elements, the most difficult to work with, especially when only a few atoms are available at a time for analysis. After three years of bombarding uranium with neutrons, Hahn and Meitner were able to identify nine different radioactive substances.

The young and gifted chemist, Fritz Strassman, was brought in to help identify their infinitesimal samples. Clara Lieber, an American chemist from St. Louis, and Irmgard Bohne, a German lab technician, also came on board to form what was indisputably the most experienced group in the world studying the problem at the time.

For four years, Meitner's team and other scientists had been splitting uranium atoms without knowing it. They had not been in search of "fission;" they were looking for the transuranium elements. The scientific community knew that an atom could change gradually by losing or gaining protons; but that atoms could be divided into two equal parts was a concept completely foreign to them. The puzzle was almost solved on a number of occasions. Strassmann showed Meitner a mid-sized atom of barium, evidence that the atom actually split in two, but Meitner dismissed the results accusing Strassmann of sloppiness. Ida Noddack, a Berlin scientist and Lise's good friend, also found a mid-sized atom and concluded that the uranium nucleus could split into two parts. Her conclusion was quickly rejected by everyone, including Meitner. Even Einstein had said: "There is not the slightest indication that the energy [in the nucleus] will ever be obtainable. It would mean that the atom itself would have to be shattered, or dissolved."

It was 1936 when Nazi Germany established strict anti-Semitic laws that banned "Jewish physics." Thus, at the height of her career, Lise Meitner was banned from teaching, attending colloquia, publishing, and lecturing. Hahn was forced to omit Meitner's name from papers they had worked on together. While lecturing, he could not even mention her name. Despite the ominous political climate, Meitner's friend Max Planck urged her to stay at the institute when other opportunities abroad arose. Lise agreed, surmising that she was an Austrian and "too valuable to annoy."

When Germany took over Austria in 1938, Meitner became a German citizen overnight, a Jewish German citizen. Predictably, pressure mounted to fire Lise from the Institute. The violently anti-Semitic policies of the new government created a tension that was palpable. Hahn, who was anti-Nazi, found himself in a precarious situation and advised Lise not to come to the Institute anymore.

On a tip from the office of secret police, her friend and Nobel Prize winner Max van Laue informed Lise that no university graduates would be allowed to leave the country. The minister of education stated: "It is considered undesirable for well-known Jews to travel abroad where they appear to be representatives of German science or where their names and their corresponding experience may even demonstrate their inner attitude against Germany."

Dutch friends made an arrangement with the Dutch government to admit Lise Meitner without a visa. Professor Dirk Coster concocted a clandestine meeting in Berlin to escort Meitner to the Dutch border. She packed two small suitcases and left everything else behind in the lab. On the train she was confronted by a Nazi military policeman who studied her illegitimate Australian passport. He left for ten minutes, returned, and handed her passport back without saying a word.

After a short stay in the Netherlands, Meitner accepted a position with Niels Bohr, the renowned Danish theoretical physicist, at his Copenhagen institute. Meitner did not remain long in Copenhagen after officially resigning from the Kaiser Wilhelm Institute. She moved on to the Research Institute of Physics in Stockholm to work with Nobel Prize winning Swedish physicist, Manne Siegbahn. She later deeply regretted her decision to leave Copenhagen, as she wrote to Hahn in 1938:

> I have none of my scientific equipment. For me that is much harder than everything else. But I am really not embittered - it is just that I see no real purpose in my life at the moment and I am very lonely . . . Work can hardly be thought of. There is [no equipment] for doing experiments, and in the entire building just four young physicists and very bureaucratic working rules . . . [Siegbahn is] not at all interested

in nuclear physics, and I rather doubt whether he likes to have an independent person besides him . . . I often see myself as a windup doll, who does something automatically with a friendly smile, but has no real life in her.

Meitner remained in contact with Hahn; she was in essence still the leader of the Berlin team. Hahn and Meitner collaborated by letter almost every other day. After reading Irene Joliot-Curie's latest paper, Hahn and Strassmann decided to explore the collision debris for radium. Hahn eventually traveled to Copenhagen to consult with Bohr and Meitner. Meitner told Hahn to produce more evidence. Because, as Strassmann wrote later, Meitner's opinion and judgment carried so much weight with the men in Berlin, they immediately undertook the necessary control experiments.

The Berlin team thus went back to work to produce irrefutable evidence. On December 19, 1938, Hahn noticed that the collision had produced mid-sized atoms that paralleled the element barium. He wrote to Meitner asking her for a possible explanation of the phenomenon. In response, she did not dismiss the possibility of a process that goes with slow neutrons and leads to barium. She noted that there were often surprises in nuclear physics, so it was imprudent to say without further consideration that the barium scenario was impossible. Strassmann and Hahn sent a paper with their results to a German scientific journal. It was published on January 6, 1939. The article was strangely vague and indirect. Many believed the authors did not understand what they had found. As it turns out, they did not.

Meitner was consumed with the Berlin project. If uranium changed into barium, then all their earlier work had been wrong. During the New Year holidays, she discussed the problem with her nephew, Otto Robert Frisch, who also worked at the Research Institute of Physics in Stockholm. While out on a walk with Frisch, Meitner contemplated the characteristics of the elements in question: uranium had 92 protons, barium had 56. She mused how a neutron, normally able to chip off one to two protons, could lose 36 protons. Finally, it all made sense to Lise. The uranium nucleus which resembled a liquid drop with thin walls around it, actually split in two when struck by a neutron. They had not found transuranic elements but rather two different elements; the uranium formed elements with protons equaling 92. Sitting on an old tree, Frisch and Meitner worked out the calculations on bits of scrap paper. When the uranium nucleus breaks in two it releases over two hundred million electron volts. They were astounded at the thought. Nuclear fission was born.

Frisch hurried off to his lab to explore the biological process of cell division with a Geiger counter. By the next morning he had acquired physical evidence of the splitting of the uranium nucleus. He excitedly told Bohr of the discovery and Bohr promised not to speak with anyone about it until Meitner and Frisch published what they had uncovered in their now famous report "On the Products of the Fission of Uranium and Thorium." When a fellow scientist on board a boat to the United States told Bohr he thought the paper had recently been published, Bohr revealed one of the greatest discoveries of the century. The news in the U.S. spread within days. No one really knew whether the concept of fission would be of any practical use, but it would nonetheless change the field of science forever. Although, as Frisch later stated, "the specter of a bomb was there," it seemed impossible with such a scarcity of the correct uranium isotope.

Meitner remained in Sweden during the war. She could continue to work on fission under Manne Siegbahn. Allied forces did offer her a position to explore the possibilities of an atomic bomb, but she refused. Hahn, although anti-Nazi, stayed in Germany and served on nuclear reactor committees. In 1945, as Hahn later wrote in his autobiography: "A small detachment of American and British soldiers, accompanied by a tank, appeared at the Institute and invited me . . . and Max van Laue to come along with them. The ranks were later swelled in Berlin by Werner Heisenberg . . . we finally arrived at a beautiful country house near Cambridge, where we were well treated."

On August 6, 1945, Lise Meitner heard of the unthinkable horror — an atomic bomb, designed with the fission of uranium atoms, had been dropped on Hiroshima by the Americans. The missile equalled 20,000 tons of TNT. There had been a clandestine race to create the atomic bomb through nuclear fission. Newspapers reported on the secret details of the grisly race between Germany and the Allies to find a weapon so destructive that it would insure absolute victory. The Americans had built three immense compounds in Oak Ridge, Hanford, and Los Alamos and hired thousands of technicians and scientists to invent "the Bomb." Lise only found out after the Hiroshima bombing that Frisch and Bohr had assisted the Allies in Los Alamos. Fortunately, the Nazi Reich lost the race to build atomic power, primarily because Hitler failed to recognize the potential of fission.

Reporters swarmed Meitner after the initial broadcast of Hiroshima. In an interview with the *Saturday Evening Post*, she claimed: "I myself have not worked on the smashing of the atom with the idea of producing death-dealing weapons. You must not blame us scientists for the use to which war technicians have put our discoveries." In a radio broadcast with Eleanor Roosevelt, she stated: "I hope the construction of the atom bomb not only will help to finish this awful war, these wars here and in Japan, but that we will be able to use this large energy release for peaceful measures." Armed with this reasoning and a strong sense of idealism, Lise Meitner was able to make peace with herself.

The Nobel committee never considered bestowing laurels on Lise Meitner for splitting the uranium atom. Otto Hahn alone received the Nobel Prize in chemistry in 1944 for his work in nuclear fission. Almost all physicists agreed that Meitner should have shared the award as she had initiated the experiment and explained the process. As one German writer explained: "Lise Meitner's lifelong scientific accomplishments were crowned by the Nobel Prize for Otto Hahn." Many believed Meitner was not considered because Manne Siegbahn, who along with other Swedish physicists, controlled the physics Nobel, rejected her Nobel nomination.

A bitter competition arose between Hahn and Meitner during the ensuing years. Hahn maintained that she did not contribute to the fission of uranium. He never even mentioned her name or their 30 years of collaboration in his Nobel acceptance speech in 1946. Hahn insisted that chemistry, not physics, had solved the problem. Later he became somewhat of a hero and his picture appeared on buildings, medals, stamps, and coins. Although Meitner created the fission theory within one week of receiving Hahn's hard data, her vital contribution was overshadowed by Hahn's self-promotion. Lise was not so much hurt by her failure to secure the Nobel Prize as she was by Hahn's ignominious behavior.

Although she never complained about her lack of recognition, she was infuriated by the war-time monstrosities and Hahn's lack of Nazi resistance. She wrote:

I do not think they comprehend just what fate has befallen Germany through their passivity. And they understand even less that they share responsibilities for the horrible crimes Germany has committed . . . How shall the world trust a new Germany when its best and intellectually most prominent people do not have the insight to understand this and do not have a burning desire to make whatever amends possible?

In 1947, Strassmann offered Meitner her old position as director of the Institute, renamed the Max Planck Institute for Chemistry. She declined with a wrathful contempt for the country that had killed millions of innocent people. In response to Strassmann, she wrote: "Germans still do not comprehend what occurred, and they have forgotten all atrocities that did not personally happen to them. I think I could not breathe in such an atmosphere."

Only occasionally returning to Germany after the war, Meitner remained in Sweden for 22 years. Before she retired from research at age 81 and moved to Cambridge, England, the accolades slowly poured in. In her typically humble way, Meitner never talked publicly or privately about the 1946 Nobel Prize, her emigration from Germany, her hardships, or her struggle for acceptance. She never wrote an autobiography or authorized a biography. She did, however, preserve all of her data. She left behind a vast collection of notes and all of Hahn's letters; she left behind the real story.

The woman who propelled the world into the Atomic Age passed away at the age of 89. She was one of the greatest experimentalists of her day who contributed to both the experimental and the theoretical sides of nuclear physics. Buried in Hampshire, England, her headstone reads: "Lise Meitner: a physicist who never lost her humanity." That is undoubtedly how Lise would have liked to have been remembered. More than anything else, Lise Meitner hoped that uranium fission would be used for peaceful purposes. Indeed it has, as nuclear fission has made many things, such as moon probes, possible today. She ended most of her lectures by saying: "Physics has brought light and fullness into my life." In return, Lise Meitner gave light and fullness to the world.

Chapter 8

ഇഡ

Amalie Emmy Noether

Amalie Emmy Noether came from a middle-class Jewish-German family. Neither conventionally pretty, nor particularly rich, nor interested in the conventional role of women in her society, Emmy would forge her own destiny into history. She would become known as the originator of a new kind of algebra, and she would lead the way for mathematicians and scientists to view the world in a new light.

Amalie Emmy was born in 1882 to Max and Ida Noether in Erlangen, Germany. Although born to Jewish parents, Emmy inherited a non-Jewish family name due to a series of Prussian laws instituted in the early half of the nineteenth century that required Jewish citizens to change their family names and bring them into accord with Germanic regulations.

Her father Max was born in Mannheim, Germany to Hermann and Amalia Noether in 1844. At a young age he suffered the ravages of infantile paralysis which, after a long recovery, left one of his legs crippled. Max came from a line of merchants who had established a successful iron wholesale firm in the late 1830s, and his family was financially able to provide the recovering child with the best private tutors. Max studied literature, history, and astronomy as a young boy, and obtained a Ph.D. from the University of Heidelberg in 1868. At school he had focused on

Source: Bryn Mawr College Archives

the mathematics of geometry. He followed this passion to Erlangen where Felix Klein had established a world-prominent program based on his unifying theory of various geometries.

Emmy's mother, Ida Amalie Noether, née Kaufmann, was born in 1852 in Cologne as one of ten children. Her family was also well-off and Jewish. Emmy would have a much smaller pool of siblings surrounding her. The first child born to Max and Ida, Emmy was followed by three brothers, Alfred, Fritz, and Gustav Robert.

Emmy's destiny as one of the world's most gifted and profound mathematicians was partially inherited from her father. Max had chosen an academic career instead of following his family history and becoming a merchant. He was a full professor at the Erlangen University and a world-famous theorist, having devised an important algebraic geometric theorem known today as Noether's Fundamental Theorem. This work would be his most important contribution to the world of mathematics. He spent the remainder of his years working on supplements to this early research, but his legacy as a mathematician would live on in Emmy as she took her place among the mathematical geniuses of the world. In fact, she developed some of her own important work based on her father's original theorem.

As a child, Emmy received what was a standard education for a young girl from the comfortable burgher class. She attended the Stadtischen Hoheren Tochterschule for eight years, while also receiving extracurricular education in household duties from her mother and taking piano lessons. At school, Emmy was particularly good at language studies, especially in French and English. This led her to take the Bavarian State Examination for teachers of French and English in 1900. After five days of testing, she passed with excellent scores, earning the right to teach at female education institutions. But that would not be Emmy's future.

Influenced by her father's passion for mathematics and constantly surrounded by his colleagues, especially his close friend Paul Gordon, who was also a mathematics professor at Erlangen, Emmy chose a more rebellious and ambitious route. She decided that she wanted to attend the university.

In 1900 Germany, Emmy's decision was decidedly against the common social wisdom. At the time it was widely held that women would be a disruptive and corruptive presence in university lectures and classrooms; university boards and professors routinely denied the few requests from potential female students to enroll in, or even audit, the classes. But due to her father's influence at the university, Emmy was able to audit classes at Erlangen. She attended Erlangen for two years. In 1903, she passed her matura examinations in Nurnberg. From there she proceeded to Gottingen, a university that was gaining prominence as one of the primary theoretical mathematics centers of the world. It would, in the coming years, build on that reputation to become a focal point of the newly developed science — quantum physics. Emmy studied in Gottingen for only a semester because she returned to Erlangen immediately when she learned they had officially granted female students the same rights as male students. She graduated on October 24, 1904.

Emmy was, by then, firmly determined to continue her academic path. She spent three years working on her doctoral dissertation under her father's friend, Paul Gordon. She would be Gordon's only doctoral student during his career. Her dissertation, "On Complete Systems of Invariants for Ternary Biquadratic Forms," was accepted and registered in July of 1908. Based on this work, Emmy was able to obtain a non-paying position at the Mathematical Institute in Erlangen. Although her gender left her penniless and dependent, Emmy was able to use her position to continue her own research and to interact with other mathematical theorists. She would also occasionally substitute for her father at his lectures. She held this position for seven years, earning during that time membership in both the Circolo Matematico di Palermo and the Deutschen Mathematiker-Vereinigung. Emmy was excited by her membership in these two organizations, and she attended meetings and gave presentations quite frequently.

While she was working unpaid in Erlangen, Emmy's influences shifted. She had been a student of Gordon's, drawing heavily on his computational style of mathematics in her thoughts and studies. When he retired, soon after Emmy had earned her Ph.D., Emmy began to engage Ernst Fischer. They frequented mathematics seminars together and maintained ongoing discussions and correspondence about mathematical theory. Through Fischer, Emmy learned to take a more abstract approach to mathematics, a skill that prepared her for her work on the groundbreaking theories of Albert Einstein. In her most important paper written while at Erlangen, Emmy's notes indicate that the work was inspired by her discussions with Fischer. Emmy became so proficient at the Fischer style of the invariant theory of mathematics (the study of solutions of systems of equations) that in 1915 she was invited by the prominent mathematicians David Hilbert and Felix Klein to join the mathematicians who were gathering in Gottingen to work on the new physics inspired by Einstein's ideas.

In Gottingen, Emmy became particularly interested in the connections between differential invariant theory, the application of which allowed highly complex and specific theories to be expressed in more simplified terms. Emmy was so proficient at this abstract, generalized approach to mathematical solutions that, in 1918, Einstein himself commented on her work in a letter from May 24:

> Yesterday I received from Miss Noether a very interesting paper on invariant forms. I am impressed that one can comprehend these matters from so general a viewpoint. It would not have done the Old Guard at Gottingen any harm, had they picked up a thing or two from her. She certainly knows what she is doing.

Yet Emmy's gender still hampered her professional standing, even though she was well respected and welcomed by her peers in Gottingen. Hilbert and Fischer attempted to get her a better position than she had had at Erlangen. Their efforts were only nominally successful, and their vocal support of Emmy put them at odds with the board. They attempted to get her a position as Privatdozent, a non-paying position that would allow her to lecture under university sponsorship. But this position was available only to males, and the university felt it would be socially detrimental for soldiers returning from World War I and attending university to be instructed by a woman. Hilbert also attempted to file a special petition for compensation on Emmy's behalf, which was roundly rejected. Eventually, the university acquiesced and allowed Emmy to lecture, but only under Hilbert's name.

Under the auspices of Hilbert, Emmy continued her research into differential invariants at Gottingen. By the spring of 1919, the war was over, the political climate had shifted, and Emmy's chances for gaining her own position at Gottingen greatly increased. She was allowed at this time to apply for the position that had been denied her previously. In her seminar delivered to the faculty as a bid for Privatdozent, Emmy listed her already long list of achievements and spoke specifically about her most recent work with Hilbert and Fischer on aspects of Einstein's general theory of relativity.

This work finally won her a position at Gottingen, but this was only the first leg of Emmy's impressive journey into history. The Russian topologist, P.S. Alexandroff, would say of Emmy Noether's importance:

> When we speak of Emmy Noether as a mathematician . . . we mean
> not so much these early works, but instead, the period beginning about
> 1920 when she struck the way into a new kind of algebra.

In 1920 Emmy published her first major paper in the journal *Mathematische Zeitschrift*. In this paper, Emmy introduced the algebraic concepts "right ideal" and "left ideal," and expanded these into a more complete consideration of the general theory of ideals in a paper that appeared in *Mathematische Annalen* the following year. Weyl said of this publication: "It is here for the first time that the Emmy Noether appears whom we all know, and who changed the face of algebra by her work."

While she was busy rewriting and expanding algebraic concepts, Emmy's professional advancement continued to be stalled by a sexist society. In April 1922, the Prussian Minister for Science, Art, and Public Education conferred upon Emmy the "title" of Unofficial Associate Professor. She would have a title in name only; she was given no responsibilities and still received no salary.

In 1924, a student arrived in Gottingen who would become one of the most vocal and important proponents of Emmy's theories. B.L. van der Waerden, a child prodigy in mathematics, responded quickly and deeply to Emmy's research. In 1931, he published a book now famous among mathematicians, entitled *Moderne Algebra*. More than half the book was based on Emmy's lectures at Gottingen.

The period of the late 1920s was an exciting time for Emmy. Under the direction of Fischer and Hilbert, Gottingen secured and expanded its reputation as the world's center of mathematics. Key mathematicians from all over the world traveled to Gottingen, sometimes for brief visits and lectures, and sometimes to assume positions at the university. Emmy was at the center of this hotbed. She earned a strong and enduring reputation among her colleagues both for her original and exciting theories, as well as for her unconventional ways. Emmy was not a women concerned with the feminine trappings of her society. She did not spend time on primping or dress, and she was said to be loud, argumentative, and passionate about the only thing that really mattered to her — mathematics.

In 1932, Emmy received two honors that would be among the highest forms of recognition she received in her life. She was awarded the Alfred Ackermann-Teubner Memorial Prize for the advancement of mathematical science. The prize included a cash award of 500 reichmarks.

She was also named as a major address speaker at a general session of the International Mathematical Congress to be held in Zurich. From more than 400 participants, she was one of only 21 who was elected to give a major address. But this period of idyllic communion with her fellow mathematicians swiftly ended, and Gottingen's hard-earned reputation as the proving ground of modern mathematics was destroyed when the Nazis came to power in Germany.

It started in early 1933 when Adolf Hitler was named Chancellor of the Reich. By the end of spring, university students, newly empowered by the Nazi movement, began to appear on campuses wearing SA uniforms (the brown-shirted uniforms sporting swastika armbands which were the dress for students supporting the Nazi movement), boycotting lectures by Jewish professors, and intimidating non-supportive students into submission. In April of that year, Emmy received a letter withdrawing her right to teach at the University of Gottingen.

Word regarding the fate of non-Aryan intellectuals in Germany spread quickly through the world. Fortunately for Emmy, forces were at work to rescue some of the deposed scholars of Nazi Germany. Her reputation as one of the leading and most original mathematicians of her day ensured her survival. In July 1933, the President of Bryn Mawr College wrote to the Rockefeller Foundation in New York to request a grant in the amount of $2000 to supplement a $4000 salary specifically arranged to attract Emmy to the college. Less than a week after Bryn Mawr sent its request to the Rockefeller Foundation's New York office, Oxford University made a similar, though independent, request to the Paris office. Soon a flurry of correspondences ensued between the Paris and New York offices and the two schools, which amounted to a virtual academic bidding war that Emmy resolved by accepting the appointment at Bryn Mawr in September.

Emmy, though not particularly interested in the mundane tasks of teaching undergraduates, became a respected and valued member of the Bryn Mawr faculty. Mathematicians from all over the country came or were invited to hear her speak. She made frequent trips to Princeton to be in the company of other theoretical mathematicians and members of the scientific community.

In 1934, Emmy joined the American Mathematical Society. Through her contact with members of the Society, a campaign was started to secure for Emmy a permanent, well-paid position in the American academic world. Solomon Lefschetz wrote the following letter regarding Professor Emmy Noether's place in the mathematical world:

She is a holder of a front rank seat in every sense of the word. As the leader of the modern algebra school, she developed in recent Germany the only school worthy of note in the sense, not only of isolated work but of very distinguished group scientific work. In fact, it is no exaggeration to say that without exception all the better young German mathematicians are her pupils. Were it not for her race, her sex and her liberal political opinions she would have held a first rate professorship in Germany and we would have no occasion to concern ourselves with her. She is the outstanding refugee German mathematician brought to these shores and if nothing is done for her, it will be a true scandal.

By April 1935, the campaign proved successful. Bryn Mawr agreed to absorb Emmy Noether permanently into its faculty, and the Rockefeller Foundation committed to grant support for Emmy's salary. But their valiant efforts and success would never be instituted. Within a month, Emmy Noether was admitted to the hospital to surgically remove an ovarian cyst. Four days after the surgery, Emmy lost consciousness and never recovered. Doctors blamed the cause of death on a stroke, but a virulent infection was more likely. She was buried on the campus of Bryn Mawr.

Emmy Noether's life serves as an example of the great victories and achievements that can be gained through dedication and perseverance. She never lost sight of her goal to elicit the truths of a new mathematics. Her efforts are felt not only in the theories she originated, but in the mathematicians and scientists whom she and her work inspired.

Chapter 9

෨ාൠ

Leta Anna Stetter Hollingworth

I n the spring of 1886, just after midnight, Margaret Elinor Danley
Stetter gave birth to her first child. She would chronicle her child's
first year of life in a diary she kept especially for that purpose, and wrote
in it as if from the child's point of view. Of the birth, she recorded these
events:

> I was born May 25th, 1886, Tuesday morning at 12:30 . . . [Mamma]
> took me in her arms, kissed me, and said, "A little girl; isn't she
> sweet?" [A week later] I heard Grandma tell Mamma that she saw
> somebody walking up the road with a white hat on. Mamma said,
> "Maybe it's Johnnie." Then I heard the door open — a man came in,
> walked up to the bed, kissed Mamma, then took me up in his arms, sat
> down on a chair by the side of the bed and took a good look at me —
> laughed — and said, "It's the prettiest baby I ever saw." I was looking
> at him too — I had been waiting eight days to see him and now I was
> wondering how well we would like each other. I had just about made
> up my mind that I was going to love him a great deal, when he said,
> "I'd give a thousand dollars if it was a boy."

And so, it was with a cruel intermingling of appreciation and
disappointment that Leta Anna Stetter Hollingworth entered the world.
Her father's response to her birth would prove to be prophetic. Leta

Source: Nebraska State Historical Society

Hollingworth would struggle her entire career to overcome obstacles simply because she was a woman. She, as did many progressive and intelligent women of her day, waged war against such prejudices until her death. Leta Hollingworth became the first clinical psychologist in New York City and, through her research, redefined the understanding of the psychology of women and children with extraordinary IQs.

In later years, Leta would describe her childhood as a "fiery furnace." From an early age she learned to face her life struggles with strength and resolve. She was born to a homesteading family in the White River region of Nebraska. Her father, John Stetter, descended from Black Forest Germans. As a young man, he moved from his Virginia home to Nebraska, seeking fortune and freedom in the Midwest. He was a slick and charming man, but he was also a drunk and a ne'er-do-well. He took temporary jobs that kept him away from home, such as cowboy, peddler, and entertainer. Although these pursuits reveal his sense of adventure, which Leta seemed to inherit, he lacked the focused mind, the determination, and the compassion that became Leta's hallmarks.

Little is known of Leta's mother, other than she was from a family of Scotch-Irish Presbyterians who had journeyed to Nebraska from Illinois to seek out life as homesteaders. She died three years after Leta was born due to complications with the birth of her third daughter. Leta and her two sisters were sent to live with their maternal grandparents.

When Leta was twelve, John Stetter remarried and recalled the children to his home in Valentine, Nebraska to be raised by their new stepmother. By Leta's accounts, her stepmother was a strict and violent woman, given to uncontrollable bouts of rage. It was so bad that Leta devoted nearly all of her energies to escaping the terrors of homelife. She even made what she would later call a "solemnly kept compact with life: that if I left out part of childhood I should be granted other values which seemed more to be desired . . . I decided to grow up then and there, solemnly renouncing the rest of childhood . . . Nor has life failed thus far to keep up the compact." The sense of isolation in her own childhood was reflected in her later work, as she studied and redefined the plight of gifted and retarded children in a society that was as strict and inflexible with the education of its children as her stepmother was with Leta and her sisters.

In 1901, Leta graduated from Valentine High School. The following year she entered the University of Nebraska to study literature and creative writing. She had been drawn from an early age to literary expression.

At the age of fourteen, she had a poem published in her local newspaper. At the University, her talent and determination won her many honors: she was a contributing literary editor of *The Daily Nebraska*, an associate editor of *The Sombrero*, and assistant editor of *The Senior Book*. Destiny, however, had a different path chosen for Leta.

At the University, she met and fell in love with a young psychology student named Harry Hollingworth. In 1943, he wrote the following anecdote about his first visions of her:

> She used to frequent a remote stack room in the library, where the heavier volumes on anthropology, philosophy, psychology, and social science were shelved. Usually this room, if peopled at all, contained worried adult graduate students working on theses and a few unduly sober majors in philosophy and psychology. I first observed her on her frequent visits to these somber quarters wearing a bright scarlet Tam-O-Shanter on her dark hair, and poring over one or another of the giant tomes. She brought a new and brighter note into the dusty stack room.

In 1906, Leta and Harry graduated from the University. Harry moved to New York to attend graduate school at Columbia. Leta remained in Nebraska. She had intended to make a career as a writer, but had taken the precaution of earning a teacher's certificate at the University, in addition to her literature degree, so that she might support herself until she "made it." After two years of teaching in Nebraska, and receiving no response from her short story efforts, Leta moved to New York City to marry Harry Hollingworth.

Leta intended to continue teaching once there, but a New York City regulation prevented married women from teaching. The Hollingworth household was forced to endure financially hard times due to this unrealized income and Leta, now forced into a life of purely domestic pursuits, became despondent. She applied to graduate programs in literature, but no scholarships or grants were available for women seeking the highest levels of education, and she could not afford tuition. It was during this time that Leta's dream of becoming a writer died, and Leta began to realize that the role of a woman in this society was limited both legally and socially. The frustration she felt at being limited to a domestic life fueled the next stage of her life. Leta reemerged as a psychologist, a feminist, and a revolutionary.

In 1911, the Coca-Cola corporation was being sued by the U.S. Government for marketing a caffeine beverage. Caffeine, the government held, was highly detrimental to a human's health, especially its impact on mental capacity and general performance. Coca-Cola decided to establish a research grant that would make use of the relatively new field of applied psychology to conduct studies that would hopefully disprove the government's claims. The grant was given to Harry Hollingworth, one of the most notable applied psychologists of the day. Harry hired his wife to direct the study. As one of the first commercial uses of applied psychology, Leta's work on this project displayed exemplary scientific standards and well-designed, rigorous study. It also disproved the government's claims, and the Coca-Cola corporation forwarded a generous stipend to the Hollingworths for their work. With this money, Leta was finally able to escape her domestic confines.

Leta entered Columbia University in 1911 and received an M.A. in education and sociology in 1913. It was during this time that Leta began to recognize her life's calling to use science to debunk social myths that kept certain groups (women and children of non-standard intelligence) oppressed and limited in their social roles. She began first with women.

Leta herself, as an ambitious and intelligent woman, had already suffered under an oppressive, patriarchal system. She had been denied gainful employment and educational opportunities because she was a woman. She began to study the foundation of this oppression. What she discovered shocked her. The forms (if not the methods) of science had been used throughout history to institutionalize the discriminatory beliefs that kept women oppressed. Through the work in her master's program, and her subsequent doctoral work (also at Columbia), she set out to dismantle two social myths that kept women "in their place."

The first myth she tackled was based on a "scientific" theory known as functional periodicity. Thanks to Hollingworth's work, this theory no longer exists. It stated that women are less capable and responsible than men because they suffer from "cyclical hysteria." That is to say, women were considered less talented, less intelligent, and less productive than men because they were "incapacitated" by menstruation. In studying this theory, Leta discovered that it was based entirely on folk-lore and "common wisdom" and not one piece of scientific evidence existed to support the theory. For her doctoral dissertation, Leta undertook the first clinical study ever to test a theory widely accepted by both scientists and the society at large.

Leta gathered together a test group of women (the variable group) and men (the control group), and studied their mental capabilities over a three-month period. If the theory of functional periodicity was true, her empirical results would reflect a cyclical drop on the variable group's mental abilities once every month, while the control group's abilities would reflect a relatively steady line of abilities. Her study proved that there was no such thing as functional periodicity. Both groups in the study, men and women, performed at the same levels of ability throughout the entire experiment. The results of this study formed the basis of her doctoral dissertation, for which she received her Ph.D. in 1916.

But Leta's battle to prove the equal abilities of women to men was not complete. The nineteenth century had left the world with Darwin's legacy, and the oppression of women was supported by evolutionary theory as well as psychological theory. Although Leta had proved that functional periodicity was bunk, a Darwinian by-product theory suggested that there were still "biological" reasons that women were inferior to men. This theory was known as the variability hypothesis. It stated that men were evolutionarily more variable than women and, therefore, in Darwinian terms, superior. The "evidence" for this was that women had never risen to social eminence. This theory proved more difficult for Leta to challenge because its testing would involve a combination of experimentation and social theory. As one of her own mentors, Edward Lee Thorndike, stated: "One who accepts the equality of typical (i.e., modal) representatives of the two sexes must assume the burden of explaining the great differences in the high ranges of achievement." Leta accepted that burden.

She first attacked the scientific reasoning behind the variability hypothesis. In her research, and through her life experience, she had discovered two things that immediately challenged the validity of the theory. First, she discovered that pre-Darwin, when a high value was placed on biological constancy rather than variability, it was commonly held that women were more variable than men. Subsequent to the acceptance of many of Darwin's theories, the theory became reversed, with no apparent scientific basis. Evolution illustrated that variability was more desirable because it allowed a species to develop and insured its survival; therefore, men were more variable. Once again, Leta was shocked at the self-serving "evidence" that was accepted by so many men. Second, she realized that there was an obvious social component that prevented women from succeeding. Thorndike had gone farther than almost any other man of science in declaring that the failure of women may to some extent be due to the difference in reproductive instincts. He also declared that:

We should first exhaust the known physical causes before we proceed to any assumption of mental inferiority in explaining woman's lack of achievement. But have these "known physical causes" been exhausted if we end with the conclusion that "the probably true explanation is to be found in the greater variability within the male sex"? Surely we should consider first the established, obvious, inescapable, physical fact that women bear and rear children, and that this has always meant and still means that nearly 100 percent of their energy is expended in the performance and supervision of domestic and allied tasks, a field where eminence is impossible.

Her next challenge would be to prove, through empirical science, that the variability hypothesis was wrong.

Leta had been hired as New York City's first clinical psychologist in 1914, based on her successful master's work and her work with the Coca-Cola study. She was working at Bellevue Hospital administering intelligence tests to patients there when she teamed up with Helen Montague, a fellow clinical psychologist, to begin an experiment that tested the variability hypothesis. She reasoned that if social conditioning was truly the factor that kept women from places of social eminence, then the best group to test for variability of traits, and nothing else, would be a group of unsocialized subjects. Leta and Helen decided to conduct tests on infants and babies. They established a group of 2,000 neonates, half of them male and half female. By studying these infants, Leta was able to prove that the variability of males was no greater than the variability of females. In fact, where increased variability did exist, it tended to favor the females.

In 1916, Leta published an article with Robert Lowie entitled "Science and Feminism," which put the variability question, at least scientifically, to rest. That same year, Leta published an article entitled "Social Devices for Impelling Women to Bear and Rear Children," in which she made her claim that the reason women did not traditionally reach places of social eminence was because they were socialized to believe that motherhood was the highest goal they should strive for and that, until society offered women the same freedom as men in choosing their destinies, the true social potential of women would never be known.

Already, Leta's career had reached tremendous heights for a poor woman from rural Nebraska in the early twentieth century. But, in the same year that she put to rest the final piece of the "woman problem," Leta's life took an unexpected turn that would lead her to make contributions to another field with an abundance of equally questionable theories: the field of educational psychology.

In the summer of 1916, Naomi Norsworthy, one of Leta's professors at Columbia, died. Norsworthy was a professor of educational psychology and her position was offered to Leta. She accepted, and devoted the rest of her career to improving the understanding of children of below-average and above-average mental abilities, and to educating these groups effectively and compassionately.

At that time, education was highly regimented, and children with unusual abilities were seen as either mental defectives, or delinquents, or both. The education system consisted of classrooms with chairs bolted in straight lines, primers, and group recitation. In this highly structured and rigid environment, children of either below-average intelligence or above-average intelligence suffered for their exceptional minds. They either fell behind and were expelled or sent to reform school, or they longed to excel beyond the pace of the class and found themselves isolated, depressed, and bored. As with her work on social obstacles facing women, Leta first had to demonstrate that it was not an inherent defect that kept children of non-standard intelligence from educational achievement, but rather an inflexible social system that catered only to the average student.

Although she also worked with children of below-average intelligence, her main efforts in educational psychology were with what we now call "gifted" children. It was commonly believed that children of above-average intelligence were, by and large, social misfits. They lacked emotional stability and could not interact well with other children or with adults. In fact, these descriptions were often true, but the belief that it was the direct result of their own intelligence was not true, as Leta discovered.

Using the same rigorous scientific method she had employed in her other major projects, Leta set about chronicling all the influences that acted upon gifted children. Not only did she measure their IQ, but she also took into account influences on social and emotional skills. She discovered that gifted children were being suffocated by an educational and social system that made no allowances for their unique abilities. Based on these early studies, Leta convinced the New York school board to initiate an experimental program that would provide a more appropriate educational environment for gifted children.

In 1936, the Speyer School opened in Manhattan and Leta oversaw the programming. She was careful to make sure that, in addition to providing a more nurturing educational environment, the school would also serve as a scientific study from which educational reforms could be modeled nationally. In addition to the students' educational progress, their emotional and social development were tracked as well. The curriculum was specifically tailored to address the needs of the students, i.e., to make the holes accommodate the pegs, rather than vice versa.

In her work with the Speyer School, Leta developed educational policies that are common today: special education classes for students of below-average intelligence, accelerated learning for gifted children, a thematic curriculum, individual student projects, field trips, and the early study of languages and arts.

To the great misfortune of the educational community, Leta died just as her work at Speyer was beginning. In 1939, she succumbed to abdominal cancer. Her final work, which her husband published posthumously from her copious notes, was *Children Above 180 I.Q.* It detailed the results she observed at Speyer and outlined the special "child-centered" learning techniques utilized to achieve those results. These techniques soon spread, and today we see their effect in special classrooms and magnet schools throughout America and the world. Leta freed the children from their blind recitation and bolted chairs.

Though her work was nothing less than revolutionary, questioning antiquated myths about the inferiority of women and how best to educate children, Leta Hollingworth was largely unrecognized in her day. She was known, if at all, because she caused strife, challenging the accepted social order. But with the exception of an honorary degree conferred on her and her husband by the University of Nebraska, and the stipend from Coca-Cola, which was paid directly to Harry, Leta never received the recognition or rewards she deserved. As Lewis Terman, a fellow educational psychologist who also studied gifted children wrote after her death, "Comparable productivity by a man would probably have been rewarded by election to the Presidency of the American Psychological Association." Despite her achievements and despite her early work on the psychology of women, Leta's gender haunted her career to the end. But her work has had unquantifiable effects on our society. Leta Hollingworth's work laid the original scientific foundations for the equality of women and respect for children — work that, to this day, is at the forefront of our social dialogue and evolution. Only today, as we begin to see the long-term effects of her work, is the world moved to applaud this indomitable scientist.

Chapter 10

ဆာလ

Gerty Theresa Radnitz Cori

In the 1850s, the eminent French physiologist Claude Bernard demonstrated that the body converts glucose into a complex carbohydrate called glycogen. The body then stores this glycogen in liver and muscle tissue until the body needs energy, at which point the glycogen is reconverted into glucose. But nobody knew exactly how the body accomplished this storage and conversion process called glycolysis until a dedicated and brilliant biochemist named Gerty Cori began to tackle the problem in the mid-1930s.

Gerty Theresa Radnitz Cori was born in Prague, Czechoslovakia, then part of the Austro-Hungarian Empire, on August 15, 1896. She was the first of three girls born to Otto and Martha Radnitz. Her father was a successful businessman who managed sugar refineries, and the family was financially well-off. Gerty and her two sisters, Lotte and Hilda, were privately tutored at home. The girls were raised in a well-appointed apartment, immersed in the art, architecture, and history of their native Prague, and enjoyed vacations on the Belgian coast. Gerty's childhood interest in the outdoors and in the arts would remain with her throughout her life.

When she was ten, Gerty was sent to complete her education at a private girls' school in Teschen, Czechoslovakia. Gerty's maternal uncle,

Source: Bernard Becker Medical Library,
          Washington University School of Medicine

Robert Neustadt, a professor of pediatrics at the University of Prague, encouraged her interest in science; and, by the time she graduated in 1912, she was intent on studying chemistry and medicine at the University of Prague. But Austro-Hungarian girls were not expected to attend the university, and Gerty's secondary education reflected this negative expectation. She had been schooled largely in the cultural and social graces. She lacked the schooling in science and mathematics which was required for entrance to the university. Gerty's early curriculum lacked eight years of Latin and five years of physics, chemistry, and mathematics. With unyielding determination, she enrolled herself at the Realgymnasium in Tetschen and completed these requirements in just two years. She took and passed a special entrance exam called a matura and was admitted to the university. She later called her matura the hardest examination she had ever taken.

In 1914, Gerty entered the Medical School of the German branch of the University of Prague, then called Ferdinand University, where she met Carl Cori in an anatomy class during the first semester. They soon fell in love. Carl was a tall, fair-haired, blue-eyed student whose family had a long history of scientists. His father was a zoologist who headed the Marine Biological Station in Trieste, where Carl had grown up; and Carl's grandfather, Ferdinand Lippich, was a professor of theoretical physics at the university where he and Gerty studied. Gerty was an energetic young woman of eighteen years who cut a tall, slender silhouette and had brown eyes and red hair. She also had a passion for scientific research that rivaled Carl's.

Gerty and Carl soon found that they had many things in common. Both of their families came from Austria. They shared a love of outdoor activities and often spent their leisure time in the country or on skiing trips. And, of course, they collaborated on their mutual first love, scientific research. Their first project was a study of human serum complement, a substance in blood involved in immunological responses. From this work emerged their first joint paper, which was published in a Czechoslovakian scientific journal and which Gerty referred to as "a modest contribution to the knowledge of the complement of human blood." Throughout the course of their lifelong collaboration, the Coris continued to make bold contributions to the world's knowledge of human biochemistry.

While they were at the university, World War I swept through Europe. Carl enlisted as a lieutenant in the Sanitary Corps of the Austrian Army.

He served on the Italian front in an infectious diseases hospital. Gerty worked as a medical assistant at the university, giving physical examinations and conducting laboratory tests.

Carl returned to Prague in 1920, and that year both Gerty and he received their M.D.s. They moved to Vienna and were married on August 5, 1920. Carl began work in the clinic at the University of Vienna and also worked in the pharmacology department at the University of Graz. Gerty found work as a research assistant at the Karolinen Children's Hospital in Vienna. She worked with patients being treated for congenital myxedema, a disease that attacks the thyroid gland, diminishes a child's mental and physical activity, and causes subdermal deposits to form, making the child's skin swell and thicken. Gerty studied these children, attempting to discover how their dysfunctional thyroids were affecting their ability to regulate temperature properly. The work was difficult and emotionally painful.

Gerty also found that her social world was becoming difficult and painful. With the end of World War I came the end of a traditional way of life for many Europeans. Over a half-dozen monarchies were destroyed, including the Austro-Hungarian Empire. The Coris now lived in a socially and economically ravaged republic of Austria. During this time, Gerty suffered, as did many citizens, from malnourishment caused by the scarcity of food in the post-war country. Carl avoided this ailment because his position at the clinic paid him with one free meal per day, rather than with money. At the Children's Hospital, officiating physicians declined a similar dietary plan which was available to them through U.S. government aid. Gerty developed a vitamin-A deficiency and was sent back to Prague, where she could obtain better food and convalesce.

Carl claimed that the war and its effects left indelible impressions on him, and he therefore felt a need to do scientific research in a place "free of strife." Gerty had also been affected by the human suffering she had watched first-hand during the war, and she made it her goal to alleviate it somehow. The Coris decided to seek out a more hospitable environment and, in 1922, they accepted an offer to come to Buffalo, New York as research scientists. It would be a major turning point in their careers. Gerty later said: "The high state of development of biochemical methods in the United States came as a revelation. The Institute offered good equipment and complete freedom in the choice of problems." It was in this environment, free of strife and armed with the latest technological advancements, that the Coris would make discoveries that expanded humanity's understanding of how the body stores and creates energy for itself.

Between 1922 and 1931, the Coris worked as researchers at the State Institute for the Study of Malignant Diseases, which had invited them from Austria. Carl was a staff biochemist and Gerty was, first, an assistant pathologist, but was later promoted to assistant biochemist. Probably owing to her work on thyroid patients in Vienna, the Institute at first tried to pressure both of the Coris to work on cancer research, but Gerty and Carl had different plans. They began in Buffalo what would become their most intimate scientific collaboration and their most important work.

They wanted to study the way animals metabolize carbohydrates, so they organized a project that focused on the way tumors metabolize carbohydrates, thereby balancing the Institute's desires with their own. However, the administrators at the Institute disapproved of the collaboration between Gerty and her husband and attempted to occupy her with separate work, which she quickly accomplished and then used her extra time to perform laboratory experiments with her husband.

The Coris often confronted this kind of pressure. When a nearby university offered Carl an attractive position, he declined because the administrators insisted he stop collaborating with his wife. On their final visit to the university, Gerty Cori was taken aside and told that she was standing in the way of her husband's career and that it was un-American for a man to work with his wife. Through the strength of their partnership and their respect for each other, the Coris withstood all such attacks on their collaborative relationship.

Around the time the Coris arrived in Buffalo, the scientists Federick Banting and John Macleod discovered insulin, a hormone that operates in the metabolic pathways of animals. Excited by this new discovery, the Coris diverged from studying carbohydrate metabolism in tumor cells, and began to study normal carbohydrate metabolism. In 1923, the Coris published their first joint paper on the metabolism of carbohydrates. This began a twelve-year string of important scientific papers describing how the hormones epinephrine and insulin, as well as certain enzymes, affect carbohydrate metabolism.

The Coris' work demonstrated three things. First, it showed that epinephrine increases the rate at which the body converts liver glycogen into glucose. Second, it showed that insulin counteracts the effect of epinephrine. And, third, it showed that epinephrine also increases the conversion rate of muscle glycogen into lactate, and that this conversion results in the formation of a hexosemonophosphate. Based on this early work the Coris would make their most important discoveries about carbohydrate metabolism.

In 1931, the Coris both transferred to Washington University Medical School in St. Louis, Missouri, where they continued their work on metabolism. Carl had been hired as a professor of pharmacology. Although her qualifications were no less than her husband's, and although the two were equal collaborators in research, Gerty was not at first made a full professor. She was instead given a position as a research assistant in the department of pharmacology. In 1946, the Coris transferred from the department of pharmacology to the department of biochemistry.

In 1936, while undertaking a closer study of the hexosemonophosphate formed when epinephrine interacts with muscle glycogen, they had their first breakthrough. It was one of the hottest summers on record in St. Louis, and Gerty was pregnant with Carl Thomas Cori, who would be their only child. Even without air conditioning, Gerty continued to come to the lab and delve into her research until the very last moment before delivering her son. During these sweltering, late days of pregnancy Gerty and her husband, studying minced frog muscle, discovered a heretofore unknown compound known as glucose-1-phosphate. This compound was called the "Cori ester," and its discovery changed the way we understand metabolism.

When the Coris began probing the deeper questions of metabolism, it was known that the body stores glucose, the sugar used as an energy source by virtually all body tissues, as glycogen in the liver and muscle tissues and that, when required, it re-converts glycogen into glucose to provide the body with energy. How exactly this conversion is accomplished was the question the Coris were asking. It was commonly believed to be accomplished by a process known as hydrolysis, in which water breaks down the complex glycogen molecules into its usable glucose components. There was a problem with this mechanism, however, because it required inordinate amounts of energy to be stored in the glycogen to fuel the water-induced chemical breakdown into glucose. The discovery of the *Cori ester* led directly to the disposal of this old theory.

The Coris discovered that when the *Cori ester* was introduced to frog or rabbit muscle extract, it was quickly converted to glucose-6-phosphate. This compound was known to be converted into usable glucose in the body by a process called phosphorolysis, a process which uses enzymes rather than water to breakdown the compound. Working backwards, the Coris theorized that an enzyme might also be responsible for breaking down glycogen into glucose-1-phosphate, the *Cori ester*. They were able, by 1938, to isolate and discover the enzyme that satisfied this theory. This explanation of how the body circulates, stores, and converts usable glucose became known as the Cori Cycle. Although the Coris' work did not provide the definitive description of the glycolysis process, their work laid the proper foundation from which many scientists, including the Coris, were later able to document and elucidate.

In 1944, the Coris expanded their previous work on glycolysis. Using the same chemical process they believed the body used to synthesize glycogen, the Coris became the first scientists to synthesize glycogen in a test tube. This successful experiment confirmed their theory that the Cori Cycle was a multiple-step biochemical pathway through which the body interconverted glycogen and glucose. They had disproved the old theory that the body uses water to convert carbohydrates into usable and storable energy, and replaced it with a more complex, but more accurate theory that the body uses enzymes to convert carbohydrates. That same year, Gerty's status at Washington University was upgraded from research assistant to associate professor of biochemistry.

In 1947, Gerty and Carl Cori were awarded the Nobel Prize for Medicine and Physiology, which they shared with Bernardo Houssay, who had conducted similar independent research into the role of the pituitary gland in carbohydrate metabolism. Preceded only by Marie Curie and Iréne Joliot-Curie, Gerty Radnitz Cori was the third woman, and the first American woman, to be awarded the Nobel Prize. The momentous occasion, however, was overshadowed by an unfortunate situation that only Gerty and her husband could see.

The Coris maintained an active lifestyle throughout their marriage, often taking hiking trips through the Colorado Rockies and the mountains of New Mexico. On one such trip, to Snow Mass peak in Aspen, Colorado, Gerty began to experience fatigue and pain. It was discovered that she suffered from myelosclerosis, a disease that slowly and painfully converts bone marrow into a fibrous tissue and requires frequent blood transfusions. She would live with this ailment for the next ten years. Carl remained dedicated to Gerty throughout her illness and was active in her treatment, even devising a treatment that helped her maintain relative health for a year before the side effects overwhelmed her. Keeping her illness a secret, the Coris headed for Stockholm to receive their Nobel Prize.

At the ceremony, Hugo Theorell stated that the Coris had "accomplished the astounding feat of synthesizing glycogen in a test tube" and called it "one of the most brilliant achievements in modern biochemistry." Although Gerty and Carl shared the honor of delivering their Nobel lecture on "Polysaccharide Phosphorylase," only Carl spoke at the Nobel banquet. He said: "To have thus been singled out among so many worthy scientists must evoke a feeling of humility and at the same time renew the determination to go on with the work. That the award should have included my wife as well has been a source of deep satisfaction to me. Our collaboration began thirty years ago when we were still medical students at the University of Prague and has continued ever since. Our efforts have been largely complementary, and one without the other would not have gone as far as in combination."

At the same banquet, Arne Tiselius, vice-president of the Nobel Foundation, gave a special nod to the Coris, saying: "The intricate pattern of chemical reactions in the living cells, where everything appears to depend on everything else, requires for its study an unusual intuition and a technical skill of which the Coris are masters."

After sixteen years of work for Washington University, and only after she was co-awarded the Nobel Prize for Physiology and Medicine in 1947, Gerty Cori was finally made a full professor in the department of biochemistry. She held the position until her death.

Having won the Nobel Prize, Gerty Cori was not yet done. She once stated: "Honesty, which stands for intellectual integrity, courage, and kindness are still the virtues I admire though with advancing years the emphasis has been slightly shifted, and kindness has seemed more important to me than in my youth." In keeping with that belief, Gerty turned her formidable scientific mind to the study of metabolic diseases in children. Using her unique insights into the chemical nature of glycogen and the enzymes involved in its conversion, Gerty began to study a children's disease caused by the storage of glycogen.

In 1953, Gerty Cori delivered a paper called "Glycogen Structure and Enzyme Deficiencies in Glycogen Storage Disease." She elucidated Glycogen Storage Disease by defining two types of disorders, one in which the body stored excessive amounts of glycogen and the other in which the body stored abnormal glycogen. Further, she demonstrated that these disorders were caused by either deficiencies or changes in specific metabolic enzymes. Aside from shedding light on a terrible childhood disease, this later work also demonstrated the importance of research aimed at isolating and describing individual enzymes that govern both the functions and dysfunctions of the body's metabolic processes.

In 1954, Gerty Cori announced what would be her final scientific breakthrough. It was a discovery perhaps smaller or at least less luminous than her Nobel Prize-winning work, but it appropriately capped her long years of work on the biochemical process of carbohydrate metabolism. Using the enzymes involved in its biological breakdown and conversion, Gerty Cori was able to define the molecular structure of glycogen, almost 100 years after Claude Bernard had first discovered it.

In addition to her important scientific contributions and her Nobel Prize, Gerty Cori was also recognized throughout her life with a series of scientific achievement awards. She was awarded the Midwest Award by the American Chemical Society in 1956, the Squibb Award in 1947, the Garvan Medal in 1948, and the Sugar Research Prize by the National Academy of Sciences in 1950. In 1952, President Harry S. Truman appointed her to the original board of the newly-created National Science Foundation. Her role as board member would be the only public service position Gerty ever held.

Gerty Cori died in St. Louis, Missouri on October 26, 1957. At her memorial service, a tape recording of Gerty being interviewed by Edward R. Murrow was played. "For a research worker," she said, "the unforgotten moments of his life are those rare ones, which come after years of plodding work, when the veil over nature's secret seems suddenly to lift and when what is dark and chaotic appears in a clear and beautiful light and pattern." The tape was followed by a Beethoven string quartet.

Gerty Cori once said: "I believe that the benefits of two civilizations, followed by the freedom and opportunities of [America], have been essential to whatever contributions I have been able to make to science." To that list of essentials may also be added her own special and excellent human qualities. Mildred Cohn, a student and research assistant of Gerty's, said of her: "Her mind was quick and sharp. Her enthusiasm for and dedication to science were infectious." In fact, it was so infectious that, from the pool of research assistants and students that worked in the Cori lab in St. Louis, five future Nobel Prize-winning scientists emerged.

Chapter 11

࿔

Florence Barbara Seibert

In 1900, the first wave of what would become a national epidemic of poliomyelitis swept through the small town of Easton, Pennsylvania. Caught up in this whirlwind of disease was a three-year-old girl named Florence Seibert. Like so many children who suffered from polio during the earlier part of the twentieth century, Florence's growth was stunted and she would be lame for the rest of her life. But Florence, born to what the 1942 *Current Biography* would later refer to as "an average American home of limited means," would grow beyond her handicap, as well as beyond the prejudices of the scientific world, to become a world-renowned bio-chemist who, through her work on tuberculosis and pyrogenic infections, would prove to be neither average, nor limited.

Florence Barbara Seibert was born on October 6, 1897. She was the second child, and first daughter, born to Barbara Memmert Seibert and George Peter Seibert. Her older brother Russell also fell victim to the Easton polio epidemic, but her baby sister Mabel was spared when her parents removed her from infectious proximity to her ill siblings.

Florence's father had taken over the family rug business, which gave the family a steady, middle-class income. But having three children to support would prove a constant challenge to the family's budget, especially

Source: Goucher College Archives

because of the early childhood medical needs of both Florence and her brother. Fortunately for the Seibert household, George's two brothers had both attended medical school and become doctors. When polio hit their home, Florence's two uncles came to their aid. They treated Florence and Russell and helped Barbara nurse the children through their long convalescence and physical therapy.

Due to the devastating effects of polio, especially the effect of infantile paralysis on the development of the legs, the Seiberts moved the family to a home closer to the public school, so that both Florence and her brother could more easily attend. Eventually, both siblings regained their ability to walk without leg braces or canes, and the family moved into a two-story apartment above the rug shop when Florence was in high school. Throughout this period, George and Barbara encouraged, even insisted, that their children not succumb to the deleterious effects of their childhood disease. The children were constantly encouraged to stand on their own and to play and walk with only the aid of their two legs. This challenge, to stand on one's own, would be a lesson that Florence followed unfailingly through the rest of her long and eventful life.

So completely did Florence come to believe in this lesson that even in adulthood, with a severely lame leg, she claimed only to remember her handicap when she caught sight of herself in a mirror. "That's the only time I ever seem to remember it," she would say. "And even in my forties I'm still brought up with a jolt every time I get in front of a mirror and see myself coming." Even the memories of her childhood were not fraught with terrible remembrances of pain and suffering. She would recall only that she was a normal child who grew up in a warm and loving home and that she loved to play "school" and "store" and, in an act of childhood prophecy, "doctor."

In fact, Florence's handicap did not become an issue until she approached adulthood. In high school, her lame leg kept her from attending school dances, an important social rite for young girls of the time. But Florence turned this into an opportunity for herself. She used her education in ways that girls of the early twentieth century often did not, by expanding her curiosity and her mind. She achieved excellent marks throughout her elementary and secondary school education, and she dreamed of attending college so that she would find a career that could make a difference both in her life and in the lives of others. In fact, she would later say of her early college experience: "Above all I learned . . . that I was not an invalid but was able to stand on my own two feet with a chance to make a contribution to the world."

Her efforts to achieve the dream of a college education were rewarded when, at her high school graduation, Florence was awarded the single scholarship offered to her high school by Goucher College. She accepted and moved to Baltimore to attend Goucher.

Florence's father was skeptical about her move. Although he had witnessed and encouraged Florence's growth into a woman who achieved much, he feared she might find college both physically and emotionally taxing. He insisted on going to Baltimore with her and stayed there for the first week of her classes, just in case she decided to return home. But Florence quickly proved his fears unfounded when she earned three more scholarships, made many new friends, and threw herself completely into the excitement of higher learning. George returned to Easton, leaving Florence to her own devices.

At Goucher, Florence initially studied mathematics, intending to become a teacher. The study of biology, however, began to capture her imagination and from then on she focused her attention on medicine. In her senior year, Florence announced: "I'm going to Johns Hopkins and become a doctor."

Florence's medical dreams were discouraged by most of her faculty mentors. At that time there was no Americans With Disabilities Act to ensure that public facilities were accessible to persons with handicaps, and her mentors were concerned that the life of a doctor, climbing up and down flights of stairs each day, would prove an impossible physical challenge for Florence. She ignored their advice and worked hard to complete all pre-medical school requirements. But medical school was not to be part of her destiny. The events of 1918, the year Florence graduated from Goucher, would alter the course of her life and would lead her into the scientific world, a world she had not dreamed of but would become her passion and her life's work.

World War I was raging, and all able-bodied men in America were being called to military service. This exodus created a vacuum in jobs previously allotted only to men. There were suddenly new opportunities for women to advance their careers in ways previously unavailable, especially in the industrial and commercial sciences. Florence's chemistry professor, Dr. Jessie Minor (also a woman), was offered a position as head of the laboratories of the Hammersley Paper Mills in Garfield, New Jersey. Dr. Minor asked Florence to join her as an assistant in the labs, so that Florence could earn money for her graduate work. Florence's family could not finance the enormous cost of graduate school on their modest income, especially if she wanted to attend a prestigious university, so she accepted and joined Dr. Minor in New Jersey.

Two important things happened to Florence during her time with Dr. Minor. One, she achieved what would be the first of many tastes of scientific achievement and success. She and Dr. Minor collaborated on three papers studying the chemical processes involved in the production of pulp and paper products that were published in contemporary scientific journals. Two, she discovered her true professional passion. In her own words: "I learned a tremendous lot. But mainly I learned what industrial chemistry was like and that it was not for me; that it was research I wanted." Florence followed this new-found dream with great tenacity.

Realizing that she would need new and different types of training and education to develop her passion for chemistry research, Florence decided that Yale was the place for her to receive advanced training in biochemical research. She contacted William Longley, her biology professor at Goucher, and he arranged for her to study with Professor Lafayette B. Mendel, the head of the Physiological Chemistry Department at Yale.

Though she had only meager savings to support her post-graduate work, Florence was undaunted. She applied for and won the prestigious Dean Van Meter Fellowship to help pay for her education at Yale, as well as the highly competitive Porter Fellowship of the American Philosophical Society. Of the financial obstacles to higher education, Florence would later have this to say:

> Postgraduate work is expensive. After all, not very many families can afford it when there are usually other young people waiting to be educated. But there are many scholarships and fellowships available to young women as well as to young men after they have their first degree. It was not as difficult as many inexperienced people think for me to get my first Yale scholarship for postgraduate work. And after I had that, the two fellowships that saw me through my Ph.D. came along fairly simple as a result of the kind of work I was doing. You just have to get out where you hear about these self-helps, and then ability and good work in science will do the rest for you.

Trusting in herself and her ability to do complex and thorough research, Florence completed her work at Yale and was awarded her doctorate in 1923. She was then offered dual-positions as an instructor in pathology at the University of Chicago and as an assistant at the University's Sprague Memorial Institute. It was at this institute that Florence Seibert would be drawn into the research for which she would become world-famous.

The head of the Sprague Institute was Dr. Esmond R. Long, who would become instrumental in shaping Florence's burgeoning career as a research biochemist. That year, Dr. Long received an ongoing grant from the National Tuberculosis Association to study the nature of tuberculosis and to develop new, more accurate techniques of detection, prevention, and treatment for the disease. At first, Dr. Seibert was not directly involved in the tuberculosis project. She was at work on an original piece of research for which she would garner her first major scientific award and win the respect and admiration of Dr. Long. Her research would also solve a problem that had stumped the medical field for many years.

Dr. Seibert had taken it upon herself to determine why distilled water, when injected intravenously into patients for medical and surgical procedures, caused intense fevers. The medical establishment knew that these fevers were caused by the introduction of proteins into the bloodstream, but had not yet been able to determine why triple-distilled water would create these proteins, as it was commonly understood that triple-distillation produced pure, bacteria-free water. Why, then, the so-called "protein fevers"? Through intense, deliberate, and meticulous study, as well as a fair dose of imagination and inspiration, Dr. Seibert discovered the cause as well as the solution. She determined that bacteriological by-products known as pyrogens were being transmitted into the distilled water by steam droplets. She developed a filtration system which corrected for these pyrogens and was able to solve the problem of "protein fevers" with a single distillation process. She was awarded Chicago University's Ricketts Prize for this research. A $300 award was attached to the Prize, and with that money Dr. Seibert bought herself a customized automobile. The Prize also made Dr. Long take special notice of his new assistant.

Dr. Long then put Florence to work on a particularly daunting aspect of tuberculosis research — the production of pure tuberculin for the purpose of tuberculosis detection. The journey to discover pure tuberculin had been an intractable problem that biochemists had been working on unsuccessfully for decades. Since Florence had proven her ability to solve the unsolvable through her work on "protein fevers," Dr. Long decided that she was the scientist who should work on the production of pure tuberculin. About this opportunity, Florence once said:

> Science has a lot of big men in it. And big men are quick to give opportunities to women as well as to men if they see the kind of ability a scientific problem calls for and a willingness to put into it the kind of work it needs . . . Science is not a lazy man's job — or a lazy woman's, either.

So the industrious Dr. Seibert was put to work on a problem that had eluded even the best biochemical minds.

The problem was complicated. Scientists knew that there was an active agent in raw tuberculin that caused a skin reaction in tuberculosis subjects when introduced subdermally. But the results were inconsistent. Sometimes the test would result in a positive reaction, and sometimes it would result in a negative reaction in subjects that were known to be tuberculosis positive. This inconsistency made the test unreliable for the early and inexpensive detection of tuberculosis. And without such an inexpensive technique for detection, the medical world would never be able to test for tuberculosis on a mass scale, an important first step toward the general cure of any contagious disease.

The problem stemmed from the way in which tuberculin was produced. In 1890, the biochemist Robert Koch developed what was still, 30 years later, the only method of production. Tuberculosis bacteria were allowed to grow in beef broth and the culture was then reduced through evaporation. The resulting mixture was tuberculin containing many impurities that clung to the tuberculin from the broth. Because the impurities were proteins, the process of isolating pure tuberculin seemed an insurmountable problem. Indeed, the isolation of any pure proteins was a general problem for biochemistry at the time. And until scientists could isolate and remove the protein impurities, they could not even begin to study the nature of tuberculin.

Dr. Long had already solved the basic problem of protein impurities introduced by the beef broth by developing a synthetic broth that contained no proteins. But there were still impurities clinging to the tuberculin, so skin testing remained inconclusive. Being able to remove protein impurities from the raw tuberculin also revealed another problem. Because they could now directly study raw tuberculin, scientists were finally able to discover its true nature. Tuberculin itself was a protein and, therefore, the isolation of pure tuberculin from the raw would once again have to address that most difficult task of chemistry — the isolation of proteins.

It took Dr. Seibert ten years of research to develop a method for isolating pure tuberculin. The major stumbling block was that the protein molecules varied in size, so she had to develop a filtration system that not only isolated proteins, but was able to isolate specific and varying sizes of protein molecules. She ultimately used porous clay and gun cotton to produce a creamy, white powder that was pure tuberculin. This tuberculin produced completely consistent results when used in the skin test for tuberculosis.

Because of her discovery, the National Tuberculosis Association awarded Dr. Seibert a grant to produce pure tuberculin on a mass scale. She headed a project that produced over one billion doses of pure tuberculin, more than enough to test the entire American population. So successful and accurate was her method of production that the United States adopted her tuberculin as the standard by which all tuberculin must be tested. Several years later, after defeating the World Health Organization's opposition, the National Tuberculosis Association was able to make her tuberculin the international standard as well. In 1938, the Association made Dr. Seibert the first woman recipient of the Trudeau Gold Medal of the National Tuberculosis Association.

Though this research was the crowning glory of her career, Dr. Seibert was far from done. After successfully isolating pure tuberculin, she went with Dr. Long to the Phipps Institute in Philadelphia to do field research on tuberculosis. She and Dr. Long worked on the processes of diagnosis and treatment through the research clinic they headed at the Institute, using the local population as case studies.

Dr. Seibert also began to travel the world, visiting research laboratories in Sweden, Germany, and London, where she learned about the new techniques and equipment being developed for the study of molecules. She brought this new knowledge back to the Phipps Institute and applied it to the study of tuberculin molecules. She introduced a process called electrophoresis to the United States, a process that allowed scientists to take accurate photographs of protein molecules by filtering them through an electrical field. For many years, she was one of only a handful of American scientists who both understood and could perform such studies.

In 1955, she was made full professor at the University of Pennsylvania. She held this position for only three years before moving to Clearwater, Florida. But Florence never really retired from her scientific work. She was retained as a consultant for the Center for Disease Control in Atlanta, Georgia, where she continued to work on the study of tuberculosis. During this time, she also began new research by studying the bacteria associated with malignant cancers. She continued these studies well into her eighties.

In 1963, Dr. Florence Seibert moved to St. Petersburg, Florida, where she set up a lab at Mound Park Hospital. In 1990, she was one of the first four women to be inducted into the National Women's Hall of Fame, an honor she shared with Margaret Bourke White (for art), Billy Jean King (for athletics), and Barbara Jordan (for government).

Dr. Seibert died on August 24, 1991. She will be remembered most for discovering a way to diagnose and stem the spread of tuberculosis. This amazing woman, who overcame a crippling childhood disease, demonstrated that with hard work and perseverance, an individual can stand on her own, beat the odds, and realize her dreams.

Chapter 12

ℰ)ℭ

Barbara McClintock

L egend has it that Barbara McClintock was ignored by the scientific community because she was a woman and people believed her to be "mad." But before she retired, Barbara McClintock, through sheer determination and undeniable brilliance, had climbed to the top of a profession that had at first been unwelcoming. McClintock revolutionized maize genetics with a unique blend of enthusiasm and intensity that branded her a "tiger" in her approach to her work. As one great geneticist noted: "I didn't understand one word she said, but if she says it is so, it must be so."

Born in Hartford, Connecticut, on June 16, 1902, as *Eleanor* McClintock, her parents changed her name to Barbara because her parents felt "Eleanor" was too gentle of a name for the feisty infant. Her parents, Dr. Thomas Henry McClintock and Sara Handy McClintock, had hoped for a boy and could not conceal their disappointment when their third daughter arrived. Barbara knew that her mother blamed herself for "not delivering the right thing," and sadly, Mrs. McClintock knew that Barbara knew. Their relationship would forever remain strained.

Mrs. McClintock was a Mayflower descendant who had lived an affluent life until she defied her father to marry a homeopathic physician.

Source: Cold Spring Harbor Laboratory Research Library Archives
    Photographer: Herb Parsons

She was a professional painter, writer, and pianist. Growing up in a wealthy family surrounded by servants, she was not prepared for the hard work involved in raising a family. Barbara was two and a half years old when the long-awaited brother was born. Overwhelmed, Mrs. McClintock often sent Barbara to stay with her aunt and uncle in rural Massachusetts.

Barbara had wonderful memories of her stay with her relatives. Both her aunt and uncle adored her and even talked of adopting Barbara, but Dr. McClintock refused. Uncle William, a wholesale fish merchant, let Barbara join him on his horse-drawn carriage rounds. Only a few years after Henry Ford began building cars, the family upgraded the carriage to a Ford truck. Nothing was as exciting to Barbara as when the truck broke down and she got to see her uncle fix the problem. From him, she learned both to repair machinery and to appreciate nature.

Barbara returned home at the age of six. Enthralled with insects and plants and the outdoors, Barbara spent countless hours in the back fields of their new home in Brooklyn, New York. Even at such a young age she had beautifully honed powers of observation and an insatiable curiosity. She spent most of her time alone and completely content. Barbara attributed the great sense of freedom and independence she had as a child to her parents' rejection of conventional restraints. Her parents supported all her endeavors, even those contrary to the conventional mores of the time.

At Erasmus Hall High School in Brooklyn, sports and nature gave way to a new passion — learning. Barbara loved science and math. She enjoyed solving problems, and solving them in different ways. Periodically, she mentioned her desire to continue her studies at the university level. Her mother balked at the idea, insisting that it would make her daughter "strange" and "unmarriageable." Barbara desperately counted on her father's support to attend Cornell University. But her father was in France during World War I in the army medical corps when she graduated from high school. Because her mother rejected the Cornell plans, Barbara found a job as an employment agency interviewer and spent most of her spare time studying in the public library.

When her father returned from France in 1919, he allowed his daughter to follow her dream. Within days, she was enrolled in Cornell's College of Agriculture. She felt at home at Cornell. Popular amongst her peers, she was elected president of the freshmen women's class. She also played the tenor banjo in a jazz combo that performed around town. She was a modern woman who wore golf knickers, cut her hair short, and smoked long cigarettes. Even her choice of friends was avant-garde. She had many Jewish friends at a time when the social gap between Gentiles and Jews was enormous.

By Barbara's third year of college, she was deeply consumed by science. She was fascinated by genetics and wanted to enroll in Cornell's graduate school to further explore the subject. Unfortunately, the study of genetics was taught in the plant-breeding department, where no women were allowed. McClintock therefore enrolled in the botany department and studied cytology, the study of cells.

The field of genetics was wide open at the time. Gregor Mendel's famous heredity experiment with garden peas was "rediscovered" just two years before McClintock was born. But many biologists did not accept Mendelian genetics; it was still a controversial theory describing the way inherited traits are passed from one generation to another. Scientists at Cornell were using corn, *zea mays*, as their leading research tool. It proved to be very effective as the various colors of its kernels mapped out a virtual spread sheet of genetic data. Additionally, the maize corn could be self-fertilized since each plant has both female and male flowers; female flowers contain egg cells, while the male flowers produce sperm cells, known as pollen. The pollen grain germinates, growing a long tube through a "silk" to carry sperm to the egg at the bottom of the cob.

Members of the botany and the plant-breeding department were busy staining the cells of the maize plant, attempting to uncover the differences in the ten chromosomes each plant had when McClintock tried a new staining technique and discovered how to identify and number the ten chromosomes. She could detect distinct shapes as each chromosome produced different size knobs, extensions, and constrictions. At the age of 21, she had done what no other scientists had been able to do.

Barbara's immediate supervisor was furious that the discovery was not his and others in the department simply did not understand her project. Her project did produce one fan — Marcus Rhoades. He recognized McClintock's brilliance and asked if he could work with her. Rhoades became Barbara's partner, her champion, and her best-friend. He also revealed to the arrogant male professors at Cornell the importance of her work.

Soon Barbara was the leader of the laboratory; professors and men with Ph.D.s followed her around, eager to learn. Ernest Abbe recalled:

"It was quite a remarkable thing that this woman who hadn't gotten her Ph.D. yet, or probably even her master's, had these postdocs trailing around after, just lapping up the stimulation that she provided." McClintock received recognition early in her career primarily due to Lester Sharpe, a distinguished geneticist. He introduced her research to the genetics community in his textbook *An Introduction to Cytology*.

Barbara spent just as much time in the corn fields as she did in the laboratory. During droughts, she saved her corn by laying water pipes and, during floods, she replanted her corn at night by the light of car headlights. At times, Barbara worked night and day; she was intense, fervent, and extremely driven. The harder Barbara worked the happier she was. Through brilliant experimentation, fortitude, and consistent hard work she earned her Ph.D. in 1927 at the age of twenty-five.

Barbara stayed on at Cornell as a botany instructor. She published nine papers over the next few years. Many thought her papers were milestones and that she clearly deserved a Nobel Prize for her contributions to the scientific community. Her mother unfortunately was not one of them.

Visits home were tense as her mother still hoped that her daughter would settle down and marry. She made it painfully obvious that she didn't think it was appropriate for Barbara to be harvesting corn and spending time in a laboratory. Barbara recalled: "Every time I went home at vacation time, she'd try to persuade me to let somebody go up and get my things and not go back. It was a real fear on her part that I'd be a professor."

Barbara resolved never to marry. She was simply too independent for a close, emotional relationship. She did, however, have a faithful man in her life — her undergraduate chemistry instructor, Arthur Sherburne. She admitted that "marriage would have been a disaster. Men weren't strong enough . . . and I knew I was a dominant person. I knew they would want to lean against you . . . They're not decisive. They may be very sweet and gentle, and I knew that I'd become very intolerant, that I'd make their lives miserable." Eventually, she told Sherburne not to stay in touch with her.

Together with a new graduate student from Wellesley College, Harriet Crieghton, Barbara set out to discover whether chromosomes carried and exchanged genetic information to produce new combinations of physical traits. Barbara was able to breed a special type of corn with an identifiable ninth chromosome that produced purple, waxy kernels. By examining the offspring's structure, the two researchers would be able to tell how chromosomes passed genetic information.

In the spring of 1930, they planted waxy, purple kernels from the strain. During the summer, they fertilized the silks with pollen from a plant of the same strain whose kernels were exactly the opposite, neither purple nor waxy. McClintock and Crieghton anxiously harvested the corn in the fall and made an extraordinary discovery. The ears of corn either had the usual waxy purple kernels, or were neither waxy nor purple, or they inherited one trait, but not both. Examining the chromosomes under a microscope, they found that the structures had changed — knobs and extensions had changed places. This proved that chromosomes cross over and exchange information. It was now a fact that genes were on chromosomes and that genes determined which traits are passed on to offspring.

Luckily, Thomas Hunt Morgan, upon visiting Cornell, urged McClintock to publish her findings immediately. She had planned on waiting for a second crop before publishing the data. She took Morgan's advice. Her article was published in August 1931. Only a few months later, a German geneticist, Curt Stern, published parallel data on fruit flies.

Commenting on McClintock's project, Mordecai L. Gabriel and Seymour Fogel declared in their book, *Great Experiments in Biology*: "Beyond any question, this is one of the truly great experiments of modern biology." James Peters, editor of *Classic Papers in Genetics*, wrote: "This paper has been called a land mark in experimental genetics. It is more than that — it is a cornerstone." McClintock and Crieghton's discovery became the foundation of modern genetics.

Job offers at universities and research centers did not pour in as one might have expected. Barbara had two things working against her: 1) she was a woman, and 2) she did not want to teach, but rather to immerse herself full-time in research. Although Rollins Emerson, Cornell's department chair of botany, was one of Barbara's biggest fans, he could not overrule the rest of the faculty who were opposed to giving a woman a permanent faulty position. Barbara decided to leave Cornell.

In her sporty Model-A Ford Roadster, McClintock spent the next five years driving across the country, accepting a number of fellowships usually reserved for men on their way to professorships. She received short-term grants from the National Research Council, the Rockefeller Foundation, and the John Simon Guggenheim Memorial Foundation to work at Cornell, the California Institute of Technology, and the University of Missouri.

In 1931, McClintock became the first female postdoctoral fellow at the California Institute of Technology, a men's school. On her first day there, a colleague invited her to lunch at Caltech's faculty club. When she walked in, everyone stopped eating and stared at her. They whispered about her small boyish figure, practical clothes, and tousled hair. Although Caltech usually made all visiting researchers members of their prestigious faculty club, McClintock was never allowed to step foot in the faculty dining area again.

Two years later, Barbara traveled to Germany using her Guggenheim fellowship. With Hitler as chancellor, science laboratories were in utter chaos. Her student residence was completely empty. The isolation, the political atmosphere, and the appalling persecution of Jews led McClintock to return to the United States.

Friends of McClintock's were able to arrange a two-year Rockefeller Foundation grant at Cornell University. Thomas Morgan wrote to the foundation that, "she is highly specialized, her genius being restricted to the cytology of maize genetics, but she is definitely the best person in the world in this narrow category." She received the largest income she had ever earned: $1,800 per year.

In 1936, Barbara was quick to accept a faculty position at the University of Missouri, working alongside Lewis Stadler with whom she had studied X-ray-induced mutations in maize corn years earlier. She was only granted an assistant professorship, which was far lower in rank and salary of any man with similar achievements. But is was her first real job.

As a teacher, McClintock was remembered by graduate students as a passionate lecturer, who spoke so fast that is was hard to keep up. Her sharp intellect and total command of material was clearly apparent to students, but she was usually three steps ahead of the class. One graduate student, Anna Marie Skalka, recalled: "I cannot say that I was able to follow all of what Barbara tried to communicate so enthusiastically. She seemed to think and speak largely in abstractions, a reflection, I presumed, of the classical geneticist's method of the deductive reasoning that was her primary tool." Although many had difficulty following McClintock's lectures, Gerald Fink, another graduate student, later said that her "gusto and vivacity were contagious and seemed to provide momentary rejuvenation to even the most lifeless graduate student."

According to Helen Crouse, a student who worked closely with the new professor, McClintock could be irascible with the lazy and inane. She refused to waste her time on inept students. Once Crouse asked McClintock to take a look through her microscope and when she discovered that Crouse had not adjusted the microscope properly, she stormed out of the lab and slammed the door behind her. As Crouse explained: "You had to have a pretty sturdy constitution to survive . . . [she was] the Queen Bee. Everyone was scared of her."

Her colleagues were also weary of McClintock. The University of Missouri was a very conservative and traditional institution at the time. Wearing pants, crawling through windows if she forgot her keys, letting students work in the lab past the campus curfew, McClintock was considered an agitator and an outsider. She was even excluded from faculty meetings. Crouse claims that "McClintock was absolutely furious that no one paid her any attention [professionally]." Although McClintock never publicly admitted to being bitter, she did say years later that the situation for women at the University of Missouri "was unbelievable, it was so bad." Frustrated with her rank at the University, McClintock finally asked the dean whether she would ever be offered a permanent faculty position. The answer was no, and with that she packed her bags and left the University of Missouri's botany department.

Marcus Rhoades introduced the jobless McClintock to Cold Spring Harbor in New York. It was a scientific community located on the water in Long Island. Scientists from all over the world, including Harriet Creighton, Marcus Rhoades, and Salvador Luria, flocked there during the summertime. In 1941, Cold Spring Harbor was financed largely by the Carnegie Institution of Washington, D.C. After several interviews, Barbara secured a full-time position at Cold Spring Harbor where she finally found solidarity. It was the ideal place for McClintock: teaching was not required; she had space to grow her own corn; and she had sophisticated equipment to examine the corn in a spacious laboratory. There were no restrictions on research topics; and the researchers there usually worked 80-hour weeks and wore jeans!

Working seven days a week, McClintock went back to studying her maize plants. After years of inbreeding and self-fertilization, she noticed broken chromosome problems. The plants had strange blotches of color on the leaves and corn stalks. It seemed as though every time a cell divided, chromosomes broke and genes were lost. As McClintock explained: "One cell had gained something that the other cell had lost."

She became convinced that genes were not like beads on a string, the accepted phenomenon at the time. After six years of research, she was able to prove that genes move around on the chromosome, and even from one chromosome to another. This theory explained why some offspring could have entirely different traits from their parents. McClintock called these jumping genes, "transposable elements" or "transposons."

Barbara discovered a basic genetic phenomenon that explained the wide variety of organisms produced by nature. She postulated that it "would be surprising indeed if controlling elements were not found in other organisms." Her work proved to be remarkably prescient. McClintock decided to tell the world in a paper which she sent to a scientific journal in 1951. The paper was published, but nobody paid attention to it. She tried again to relate her findings a year later at a meeting at Cold Spring Harbor for scientists from around the world. This time nobody understood her.

There were probably two reasons the speech was not a success. First, Barbara was not a good communicator. She explained things as if she were explaining them to herself. The talk, according to many observers, was extremely complicated and most could not follow her. Second, the scientific community was obstinate. They believed that genes could not jump around and thus her conclusions seemed irrational and impossible. A well-known biologist called her "an old bag who'd been hanging around Cold Spring Harbor for years." McClintock was of course disappointed, but even more surprised at the reaction of the scientific community. She later recalled: "I was startled when I found they didn't understand it, didn't take it seriously. But it didn't bother me. I just knew I was right."

McClintock published a longer, more urbane paper in 1953 and presented her results again in 1956. Geneticists seemed to accept her data by that time and regarded them with deference, but the larger scientific community still ignored her. Most believe McClintock was discounted because people simply thought she was crazy. But one colleague said this was not the case: "Most geneticists didn't think she was crazy. It was just extremely difficult both to understand her experiments and to reconcile her conclusions on transposable elements with the prevailing belief in the stability of genes on the chromosomes."

McClintock kept working on her "jumping gene" project but gave up on publishing her reports or giving lectures. As she said later: "People get the idea that your ego gets in the way a lot of time — ego in the sense of wanting returns. But you don't care about those returns. You have the enormous pleasure of working on it. The returns are not what you're after." In fact, McClintock loved working so much she hated going to sleep at night.

If Barbara was not in her lab, she could usually be found taking nature walks with a book under her arm. She kept up with all the current scientific material outside of her narrow field, regularly scanning twenty or more biological journals. She once spent an entire month reading everything on insect evolution. Other favorite subjects included Indian culture, Tibetan Buddhism, and extrasensory perception. Barbara had a keenly discerning mind with an enormous appetite and an intense curiosity about the world and its organisms.

Two decades after McClintock first presented her findings, scientists finally began to take notice of the so called "jumping gene" theory. Transposons were also found in yeast, bacteria, and fruit flies. Not until the early 1980s did the scientific community understand the importance of her discovery, which explained the many different kinds of genetic mutations that played a crucial role in evolution.

Most of McClintock's most prestigious awards came late in life. They included: National Academy of Sciences (1944); Presidency of the Genetics Society of America (1945); the Kinber Genetics Award (1967); the National Medal of Science (1970); the Rosensteil Award (1978); and the Lasker Award (1981). On October 10, 1983, she received the greatest of all scientific honors. Busy with her morning routine, she heard on the radio that she had won the Nobel Prize. Barbara would have received a personal phone call, but she did not have a telephone in her apartment. Thus, three decades after her original discovery, Barbara McClintock became the first woman to win an unshared Nobel Prize in any scientific category.

The world knew her as the "brilliant corn lady" and, after winning the Nobel Prize, she became something of a legend. Reporters swamped Cold Spring Harbor in hopes of interviewing the famed geneticist. The 81-year-old woman was courteous and always gave the press and visiting scientists her time. But she hated being famous — it interrupted her private life, and above all, it interfered with her work. She once said: "I don't like publicity at all. All I want to do is retire to a quiet place in the laboratory." In her eighties, her idea of retirement was to put in a twelve hour work day after her aerobic workout.

McClintock's last day in the lab was September 2, 1992. She died at the age of 90. Newspapers from all over the world wrote about the incredible life of the maverick, Barbara McClintock. Scientists were quoted as calling her "one of the most important figures in the history of genetics," and "the most important figure in biology in general." A colleague at Cold Spring Harbor said: "She was the most brilliant person I ever met. And she was incredibly kind and helpful to me and all young scientists. She was not only good at her own work, she was good at other people's work too." Friends remembered Barbara as forceful and strong-willed — "small in size, but great in stature," but also as someone who was warm and caring.

Today, scientists are still learning from McClintock's revolutionary concept of transposable elements. Special scientific meetings are held on the subject of jumping genes. In years to come, as scientists study evolution, genetic diseases, and cancer, her work will no doubt be at the center of their research. Barbara's 50 years of research is responsible for developing much that is considered classical genetic theory. In a tribute to McClintock, Fedoroff and Botstein write: "[S]he shook a few shoulders and more than a few minds, engendering the courage to break free and see the familiar with new eyes, rearrange the pieces in novel ways, remaining faithful only to what is really there, not the dogma of the day." The world took nearly four decades to recognize the brilliance of Barbara McClintock, a woman truly ahead of her time.

Chapter 13

&)(&

Maria Goeppert-Mayer

As a child growing up in the German university town of Gottingen during the early twentieth century, Maria Goeppert often took long "science walks" with her father. He was a respected pediatric doctor of his day and had founded and directed the Gottingen Children's Clinic. The Goeppert's were famous throughout town, both for Dr. Goeppert's work with the local children and for Mrs. Goeppert's reputation as a celebrated hostess of the most elite and exciting social gatherings. By all accounts, the Goeppert family was a model one in the conservative upper middle class society of Gottingen. So, it was odd that on one of his "science walks" with his young daughter Maria, as they stopped to classify local flora and fauna, Dr. Goeppert advised her not to grow up to be a housewife without any interests.

Half a century later, Maria Goeppert-Mayer would realize her father's advice in a most extraordinary way. She would unlock the secret core of atoms, the nature of which had eluded and confused even the most brilliant physicists. And for her discoveries, she would become the first woman awarded the Nobel Prize for theoretical physics. Later in life, recalling fondly her father's influence on her long and distinguished career, Maria said of his admonition: "Did I think it strange for him to say such things

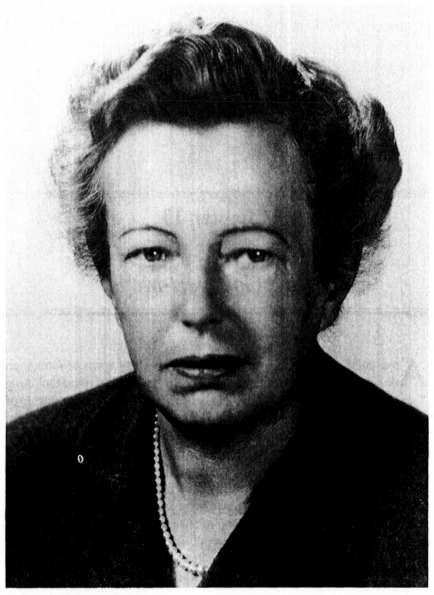

Source: AIP Emilio Segrè Visual Archives
Photographer: Louise Barker

to me? No, not at all; he could say anything to me. No, I felt flattered and decided I wasn't going to be *just* a woman."

Maria Goeppert was born on June 28, 1906 to Maria Goeppert, née Wolff, and Dr. Friedrich Goeppert in the town of Katowice, Germany. Although given her mother's name, the only child of the Goeppert family was destined to become more like her father as she made her way through the world. His influence and effect upon her was immeasurable, and his encouragement of Maria's intellectual and scientific curiosity was invaluable. Maria recognized the powerful bond with her father and embraced any opportunity to spend time with him. She considered her father interesting because he was a scientist.

But her father was not only a scientist. When Maria was four years old, Dr. Goeppert was offered a post as professor of medicine at Gottingen University, which he eagerly accepted. This would make him the sixth straight generation of university professors in the Goeppert family, a legacy to which Maria and her own children would one day add their names. Her father's appointment raised the social standing of the family in a society which highly prized rank, status, and intellectual superiority.

Maria's mother, who had come from a large lower middle class family, and who had worked as a teacher of French and piano, had settled first into the role of upper middle class housewife when she married Friedrich. After the move to Gottingen, she took up the more prestigious role of "frau professor," a professor's wife. She fulfilled her role well, becoming the most celebrated hostess in the town. When she walked into a shop, she was immediately served ahead of all other customers. She managed her house and its servants with precision and resourcefulness. Throughout her life, this image of the socially prestigious, but ultimately homebound, professor's wife would haunt Maria's efforts to achieve her scientific goals. Sometimes resented by other women, and considered an outsider by many men, especially university boards and regents, she was often under pressure to assume a more "womanly" role. Maria would instead follow her father's more independent and adventurous footsteps, although she would end up cutting a longer and wider path through the world than he.

Dr. Goeppert was an even more celebrated citizen of Gottingen than his wife. Having added to his academic success the founding of the Gottingen Children's Clinic, Dr. Goeppert attained both local and international fame. He was a rare individual who had a profound love for both his work as a children's doctor and as a scientific professor. He was a progressive thinker who believed and actively promoted the idea that children, boys *and* girls, would grow up healthier if they were not stifled, if they were allowed to be vivacious, curious, and adventurous. He disapproved of the social norm that children be raised by strict mothers who instilled in them social rules, inhibitions, and fears. He once claimed, "The mother is the natural enemy of the child."

This was the manner in which Maria was raised. Her scientific curiosity was encouraged and expanded by her frequent walks with her father. And her sense of enterprise and independence would also grow through the guidance of a father who had earned an international reputation for his unique ideas about child development. Maria came to respect him and his work so much that as an adult with her own children, she chose her pediatricians based on two simple questions: "Do you know the work of Friedrich Goeppert?" and "Do you approve of it?"

It was not, however, only her fortunate home life that would inspire Maria to her ultimate successes in life. It was also the fortunate circumstance of growing up in Gottingen. A small, medieval town which, to this day, is enclosed by a feudal wall, Gottingen had risen in the nineteenth century and early twentieth century to become world renowned as a center of cutting edge mathematics. A prestigious though obscure reputation, it would prepare its University for a great transformation in the 1920s into one of the main centers of a new and rather roguish science, quantum physics. And Maria was there from childhood on to witness, and ultimately be part of, the University's world renowned scientific achievements. But before Gottingen's elite university scientists would have an effect on Maria, she had to get her primary education. And for an upper middle class German girl, this process could easily have turned her into "just a woman."

On Maria's eighth birthday, Archduke Franz Ferdinand was assassinated, plunging Europe into World War I. Her mother's position as celebrated hostess was put on hold as all of Germany suffered through the war's food rationing. Her father's work at the clinic became a nightmare as the number of children bloated from malnutrition increased dramatically. But the Goeppert's, along with their compatriots, made the best of things. Often, families from the country would trade food, especially sausages and pigs' ears, for medical services from the children's clinic. Frau Goeppert eagerly added these war-time extravagances to the common war diet of turnip soup.

Throughout this time of sacrifice, Maria dutifully attended the public school, Hohere Tochterschule, where she excelled in languages and mathematics. But she also fell prey to minor illnesses that often kept her home. She especially remembered a year in which she suffered from migraine headaches and was only allowed to attend school for a couple of hours a day. Her father hated to see Maria's enthusiasm and education suffer from her illnesses, and he admonished her: "If you want to make yourself an invalid, you can. Don't do it." Maria, who could never resist her father's encouragement, whether it was stern or compassionate, pulled herself together and muddled through.

By the time she was in her early teens, the war ended. The Goeppert house, and all of Germany, returned to a more normal, peaceful life. Frau Goeppert again began to fill the house with party guests and dancing. In 1921, Maria entered a three year private school called Frauenstudium, a preparatory school for girls started by suffragettes. The sole intent of the school was to prepare girls for the university entrance examination. Maria recalled: "It somehow was never discussed, but taken for granted by my parents as well as by me that I would go to the University. Yet at that time it was not easy for a woman to do so." It was rather uncommon at the time for girls to be educated beyond their teenage years, when they were expected to marry and begin a family. But thanks to the encouragement of her parents, Maria would not follow in the traditional footsteps of so many German women.

After Maria had attended the Frauenstudium for a year, she and the other students received bad news. The devastation WWI had wrought on the German economy had affected the suffragettes running the school. Rising inflation consumed their finances, and they lost possession of the little house where they lived and which also served as a schoolhouse. They promised the girls to stick it out one more year in rented rooms, but after that, the girls would have to fend for themselves. To the brightest girls, the suffragettes suggested completing their prep work at the school for boys, which had just begun to admit girls. Maria did not much like the idea of attending a school of all boys and instead decided to take a bold and adventurous step. She would take the Abitur, the university entrance exam, a year early. She was cautioned against it, both for educational and political reasons. The suffragettes told her she was not ready for the exam, and she was, besides, too young to be admitted. Maria spoke with her father, and he pulled what strings he could to allow Maria to take the exam.

Maria took the Abitur in Hanover with five other girls from her school. They were outnumbered at the exam by the boys, six-to-one.

The examination was intense, covering mathematics, sciences, languages, and history. It lasted an entire week and weeded more than just a few hopefuls out of the ranks of the university-bound. But in the end, Maria's drive and dedication paid off. She was now on her way to University, where she intended to study mathematics.

When Maria entered Gottingen University in 1924, the University was in the process of being transformed from a world center for applied mathematics into a world center for the new physics that was exciting the scientific world: quantum mechanics. The famous mathematician David Hilbert had brought Max Born to Gottingen in 1921 as the chair of theoretical physics. Born, in turn, brought James Franck as a professor of experimental physics. And in 1927, Enrico Fermi came to Gottingen to study physics with Born. That year, Maria caught the physics bug that was sweeping Gottingen. She had run into Max Born on his way to deliver a physics seminar, and he invited her to attend. The seminar changed her. She said: "Mathematics began to seem too much like puzzle solving. Physics is puzzle solving too, but of puzzles created by nature, not by the mind of man." Maria switched her major.

That same year, Maria's father died. It was a tremendous emotional blow, but Maria had learned well her father's hard lessons of embracing life and staying true to one's adventurous and curious self. In memory of her father, Maria dedicated herself to completing a Ph.D., rather than simply obtaining a university teaching certificate as she had planned. Born became her mentor and supporter while she pursued her goals.

After her husband's death, Frau Goeppert began to take in borders to keep the household financially sound. Maria, absorbed in the study of physics under Born and Franck and theoretical mathematics under Heisenberg, largely ignored the comings and goings in both the house and in the German culture at large. It was a common state at Gottingen — the physicists and their students kept a safe distance from the Weimar Republic and the rise of the Nazis. But one fateful morning in the winter of 1928, Maria's mother was ill and a new tenant knocked on the door: Joseph Mayer.

Mayer was a chemistry student from America, a tan, flashy Californian whose American money made him seem rich compared to the relatively poor Germans. Joe, like Maria, had grown up with an acutely scientific mind, exploring the curiosities of nature and the mechanisms that controlled them. Unlike Maria, he was drawn toward experimental, rather than theoretical, science. He was also an active athlete who had been on the swimming team at Cal Tech. Maria and Joe began to spend time together taking walks, playing tennis, and attending dances.

The next two years were a whirlwind. Maria and Joe were married in January of 1930. Shortly after, under the guidance of Born, Frank, and Adolf Winaus, all of whom became Nobel Laureates, Maria completed her dissertation, "Elemental Processes with Two Quantum Jumps," and earned her doctorate from Gottingen. At that point, Maria's life took another major turn when Joe was offered an assistant professor's position at Johns Hopkins University. The couple sailed to America in 1930.

In America, Maria discovered how fortunate she had been to study physics in Germany. Although her rise through the University had been hard won, in America Maria learned how hard a woman of science had to struggle to carve a niche for herself in the male-dominated world of academia. Though Maria hailed from the "birthplace of quantum mechanics" and had studied under the luminary physicists of the day, Johns Hopkins refused to find an appointment for her, offering its nepotism rules as an explanation. Joe protested to the board, and finally Maria was offered a nominal salary and a dingy attic office to work as a German translator for the physics department. This was not exactly the scientific adventure Maria had envisioned. Added to her problems was the increasing tyranny of the Nazis in her homeland. Although apolitical by nature, Maria could not help but worry over the future of her people under Hitler's rule.

The scientists she worked for at Johns Hopkins quickly realized that Maria was a first-rate physicist. In fact, she was a rather exceptional one. Most physicists of the time were divided between two camps: the experimentalists and the theoreticians. Maria, however, loved to theorize and then to test her theories herself, rather than leaving the hard data work to others. She began to work with Karl Herzfeld on the quantum mechanical electronic levels of certain chemicals and dyes. At home, she and Joe educated each other in their specialties. He taught her physical chemistry and she taught him quantum mechanics.

In the summer of 1931, Maria accepted an appointment from her old mentor, Max Born. She went to Germany for the summer. The most important effect of this trip was that it revealed to her the damage Hitler had wrought in Germany and Europe. When she returned to America, she renounced with great sadness her German citizenship and became a naturalized American. The Mayer household also set itself up as a safehouse for German exiles, mostly scientists and doctors, who were fleeing Germany either out of opposition to German politics or because their lives were in danger.

In 1933, Maria gave birth to the couple's first child, Marianne. Still performing only minimal duties at Johns Hopkins, Maria decided to begin work on a book on statistical mechanics, for which she engaged Joe as co-author. It would be the beginning of a long professional relationship between them. Joe had great respect for Maria as a scientist and encouraged her to work, and to fight for the right to work, as a woman scientist. She rewarded his loyalty by making him her intellectual confidante and sounding board. Their infamous scientific wranglings and arguments inspired Maria to some of her greatest achievements.

Still working on their book, the Mayers were forced to leave Johns Hopkins in 1937. Joe had been let go under budget cuts, and accepted a position at Columbia University. The following year, the Mayers finished their manuscript, and Maria bore their second and last child, Peter. With the publication of their book pending, Maria had to contend with another aspect of her status as a woman scientist. This occurred in connection with the title page. Joe had the title "associate professor of chemistry, Columbia University" to put after his name, but Maria held no title. A sympathetic scientist at Columbia, Harold Urey, offered to let Maria lecture to chemistry students so that she might place the title "lecturer in chemistry" after her name. Despite this effort, and despite Joe's constant campaigning to have his wife recognized as an equal, *Statistical Mechanics*, which has since become a classic text still taught at universities throughout the world, was considered Joseph Mayer's work by their contemporaries.

In 1939, an announcement was made that would have a direct impact on Maria's life as a scientist. Niels Bohr and Enrico Fermi opened a conference on theoretical physics in Washington D.C. Bohr announced that at the end of 1938, two German scientists had discovered what was apparently nuclear fission. Until that point, the theoretical possibility of nuclear fission was known, but its achievement was thought to be many decades away. Now, with the Germans presumably on the verge of harnessing the immense destructive power of the atom, it became imperative for Allied scientists to begin working more earnestly on nuclear fission. It would take three years for such a project to materialize.

In the interim, Maria received her first paid teaching position at Sarah Lawrence College. In her interview, Maria had been asked by the board what type of science course she would like to teach. Drawing on her own varied experience as a scientist, she suggested they institute a class that unified the several physical science fields of astronomy (which was becoming extremely important to the new physics), chemistry, and physics. She was more than a little shocked when she was charged, as her first duty, with designing and establishing this visionary course.

In 1942, Maria received another offer, one which brought her a step closer to her fame as a scientist. Her old friend Harold Urey invited her to join a secret research team at Columbia that was connected with the nuclear fission project. At the time, Joe was also working on a top-secret project to design classified weapons systems on traditional missiles and bombs. Maria would be working on something entirely unique, something Joe believed would be the weapon of the future. Little did he, or anyone, suspect how timely Maria's project would be.

The Substitute Alloy Materials project, or SAM, was run under the strict supervision of the U.S. government, which did not discriminate against women on this project. Maria, for the first time, was given equal treatment as other scientists of her caliber. She was put in charge of a team of twenty scientists to help isolate fissionable uranium.

These final years of the war kept her and Joe separated. He was in California completing work on his classified projects, and Maria was eventually sequestered in Los Alamos, New Mexico where the final work on the world's first atomic bomb was being completed. There, Maria met up with scientists she had been friends and colleagues with for over a decade: Edward Teller, Enrico Fermi, and Niels Bohr. Maria, however, did not witness the terrifying, world-changing moment at Trinity when the world's first atomic bomb was detonated. Two days earlier, her work with SAM completed, she met up with Joe in Albuquerque and they returned to New York together. Only after Hiroshima was Maria finally able to discuss with Joe the work she had been doing for the government.

Maria returned to her position at Sarah Lawrence, but her return was short-lived. Joe was offered a full professorship at the University of Chicago. To her great surprise, Chicago also offered Maria her first associate professorship, although, citing nepotism rules, they could not offer her pay. Nonetheless, she would be an equal among her colleagues. Fermi, Urey, and Franck were working on a project initiated by Fermi and housed on the Chicago campus: the Institute of Nuclear Studies. Maria was admitted to this elite group of scientists, and her relationship with them in this new field of study would transform her into a potential Nobel-quality scientist.

After about a year of working at Fermi's institute, Teller approached Maria to work with him on the question of the origin of the elements. He knew Maria's exceptional abilities as both a theoretician and experimentalist, and because Teller preferred to work on a project with another great scientific mind, she seemed a likely candidate. At the time it was believed that all the elements in the universe had been formed at the moment of creation, what is today called "the Big Bang Theory." But, the abundance of stable elements (elements that resist degrading into other elements as their unstable electron shells disintegrate) in the universe could not be accounted for under this theory. Though it later would be discovered that the elements of the universe are produced, in fact, by the immense forces of supernova explosions, Maria and Teller set to work studying the atomic nature of the elements for clues to their origins.

Maria discovered a frightening symmetry in their data. Stable, abundant elements had either 82 or 50 neutrons (subatomic particles which, along with protons, comprise the nuclei of all atoms). Teller, diverted by nuclear weapons research, abandoned the project and Maria continued alone. She accumulated data and began to encounter other recurring, constant numbers of neutrons. She began to refer to them as "magic numbers," but other than as a numerological curiosity she could not explain them. Other scientists had noticed these numbers, but they were dismissed as coincidences. Maria intuited that they might have a deeper meaning.

At the time, Niels Bohr's model of an atom's nucleus was the accepted model. It described the nucleus as being like a drop of water comprised of neutrons and protons that moved about rapidly and haphazardly and are held together by an unknown subatomic force. That model went a long way toward describing and predicting observable physical phenomenon, but it did not account for the recurring "magic numbers." Maria took a chance. She started looking for a different model of the nucleus, one that might support her data. She adopted a dismissed model for the nucleus, which described it as a series of concentric orbits, like planets in a solar system, or electrons around the nucleus itself. The problem with this model was that it contradicted the Bohr model which described the functioning of atoms in more accurate detail. Joe urged Maria to publish her findings and initial theory, which she reluctantly did in a letter to *Physical Review*. But there was much work to be done. Maria knew that something was missing from the shell model that would make it work, but she had no idea what it might be.

Then came the epiphany. Maria was discussing the problem one day with Fermi as they sat in her office. A secretary came in and told Fermi he had a phone call. As he exited the room, he turned to Maria and asked if there was any evidence of spin-orbit coupling. This offhand question triggered Maria's ideas. She sat through the rest of the day and into the evening with pencil and paper. When she returned home late, she announced to Joe that she was finally able to explain her "magic numbers."

Spin-orbit coupling was a concept that had been explored but discarded along with earlier work on a shell-model of the nucleus. The theory stated that nucleons (the generic term for the specific nucleus particles "neutrons" and "protons") exerted greater or lesser force depending on both the directions of their spin on their axes and their orbits. Only when combined with Maria's magic numbers did the concept make any real theoretical sense.

On the verge of announcing her discovery, Maria was informed that another German scientist, Hans Jensen, had developed a similar theory independently. In 1950, she met with Jensen in Germany. It was the meeting of two great minds. They agreed to complete work on the theory together in 1951, but did not complete their research for another four years because Jensen was an incorrigible procrastinator. When their book was finally published in 1955, Jensen, in deference to Maria's dedication and in recognition that most of the work was hers, insisted that Maria's name appear first on the title page, out of alphabetical order. The Mayer-Jensen model soon became the accepted model for the nucleus.

In 1959, the Mayers were both offered full professorships at the University of California, San Diego. Maria's health was starting to fail, and she welcomed the temperate climate. But only a few weeks after arriving in California, Maria suffered a stroke which left her physically weakened. During this time, Jensen actively entertained and expected that they would be nominated for a Nobel Prize for their work. Maria, however, held no such belief. A woman had never been nominated for a Nobel Prize for theoretical physics. And though the buzz throughout the scientific community confirmed Jensen's hopes, the years passed by with no nomination.

Then, at 4:00 a.m., on November 5, 1963, the Mayers received a call from Stockholm informing her that Maria and Jensen had been jointly awarded the Nobel Prize for their new model of the atom's nucleus. Maria's response was: "Oh, how wonderful! I've always wanted to meet a king." And a month later she accepted the scientific community's highest award from King Gustaf Adolf. In her Nobel lecture she observed: "The shell model has initiated a large field of research. It has served as the starting point for more refined calculations. There are enough nuclei to investigate so that the shell modellists will not soon be unemployed."

Maria lived out the rest of her days in La Jolla, teaching at the university and gardening when her health permitted. She lived a productive life, and at the age of fifty seven became the first female physicist to claim the Nobel Prize. Maria Goeppert-Mayer died of heart failure in February of 1972, having received numerous awards and honorary doctorates for her imaginative and groundbreaking physics.

Chapter 14

ℰℭ

Rita Levi-Montalcini

Rita Levi chose to add her mother's maiden name to her father's surname in order to stand out from all the other Levis in her hometown of Turin, Italy. Her ancestors were well known Israelites who had come to Italy during the Roman Empire. The Levis aided in making Turin an intellectual center for Italian unification during the nineteenth century, and after World War I they helped set up the city as an anti-Fascist stronghold. Her ancestors' contributions were significant in Turin history, but Rita would be distinguished as the Levi whose contributions were significant in the *world's* history.

Rita was born in Turin on April 22, 1909 to an intellectual Jewish family. Her father, Adamo Levi, was an electrical engineer who built an ice-making factory in Southern Italy. Rita often described him as authoritarian and domineering. He controlled all aspects of the family's life imperiously. Although Rita did not doubt her father's love for her, he nevertheless frightened her with his explosive temper. His furious outbursts were often initiated by the smallest things which earned him the nickname "Damino the Terrible," the diminutive of Adamo. As a child, Rita would turn her head away when her father tried to kiss her goodnight, sending the kiss into the air.

Source: Washington University Archives, St. Louis Missouri

According to Rita, her mother, Adele Montalcini, was "a marvelous woman — beautiful, intelligent, sensitive, artistic." Rita loved her mother dearly, but strongly resented how submissive she was. Her mother did not seem to mind that her husband controlled her which was something that Rita could not understand.

Rita grew up with four siblings. She was very close to only one of them — Paola, her fraternal twin sister. As a child, Rita preferred to be either alone or with her other half, Paola. Indeed, they often pretended to be one person.

From a very young age it was obvious that Rita had a hunger to learn. Although she grew up in the post-Victorian era that was still dominated by patriarchal ideals, Rita desperately wanted to continue her education after the standard fourth grade. She hoped one day to attend a university. Her father, however, had other plans for her. He had seen how doctoral degrees had affected the marriages of two of his aunts and decided the twins would go to finishing school and learn how to be good wives and mothers.

Rita spent several miserable and restless years trapped at a finishing school established to produce good homemakers. Her mind craved courses in mathematics, physics, biology, or Greek, but they were not offered. She attended mindless classes and was surrounded by women whose only ambition were to be good homemakers. Rita did not want to be like these women or her mother. In fact, she found the role of a wife so demeaning that she decided never to marry.

When Rita's governess, Giovanna, died of stomach cancer, Rita resolved to become a doctor. She timidly told her father this. With the greatest reluctance, he agreed to hire a private tutor to prepare her for university entrance examinations. Over the next eight months she threw herself headlong into this program which had become the very reason for her existence. She passed the requisite examinations and enrolled in the University of Turin's medical school in 1930.

Rita was delighted at the opportunity to exercise her intellect. She was wholly committed to science and set out to prove to the world that women were as intelligent and capable as men. She was one of seven female students surrounded by a sea of men at the university. She ignored all romantic advances made by the men. As Rita later declared, "I wanted to spend all my time on research . . . I didn't want any sentimental contact with other students. I didn't want any contact as a woman."

She did, however, accept an invitation to stroll through Valentino Park with a man named Guido Boni. Rita described him as "extremely tall, with a penetrating gaze, musketeer mustache and a curious way of walking, head down and always whistling a Beethoven symphony or an aria of Schubert's or Mozart's." They would remain very close, even after graduation and the war. They were engaged for some time, but Rita broke off the engagement in 1946, adhering to the vow she made long before never to marry.

Rita Levi-Montalcini would also be attracted, intellectually, to another man: Professor Giuseppe Levi (no relation). Ironically, he possessed all of the characteristics of her father that she hated. He was explosive, loud, and domineering, but unlike her father, Professor Levi admired and encouraged Rita's mental capabilities. As a brilliant histologist, he inspired Rita's expert skill in the study of tissue structure. Under his direction at the Institute of Anatomy, she mastered a new technique that involved staining chick neurons with chrome silver to highlight the nerve cells in infinitesimal detail. She studied weft-like supporting fibers in different types of tissue for her thesis.

In 1932, Rita suffered a grievous loss when her father died suddenly from heart failure. Only after his death would she come to realize how much she had loved and worshipped him. Her autobiography is dedicated to Paola and her father.

After graduating from medical school in 1936 with top honors, Rita continued to work with Professor Levi for an additional two years. She specialized in neurology and psychiatry. At this stage in her life, Rita was torn between practicing medicine and conducting research. Benito Mussolini decided for her by allying himself with Adolf Hitler. "The Manifesto for the Defense of the Race" was issued in June 1938, which prohibited the intermarriage between Jews and non-Jews, and also prohibited Jews from pursuing academic or professional careers, from studying or teaching, and from working for a state company or institution. As a result, Rita could no longer attend lectures, use the laboratories, or even visit the library. She was devastated.

In 1939, Rita accepted a position from an institute in Brussels, Belgium. Giuseppe Levi fled too. He was nearby in Liege, and they saw each other often. They talked about everything but the war. By Christmas, Rita had returned home to Turin. She was happy to be with her family but longed to work in a laboratory. Before long, Rita had converted her bedroom into a makeshift laboratory. Her brother built her an incubator for the chick embryos she planned to study again. With her binocular microscope in hand, Rita secretly went to work. Professor Levi joined

Rita's project to study problems of the developing nervous system. Rita recalls that a "master-disciple relationship" developed between them, "characterized by ever-increasing affection and esteem." They attempted to replicate an experiment conducted by the eminent embryologist, Viktor Hamburger. In an article published in 1934, "The Effects of Wing-Bud Extirpation on the Development of the Central Nervous System," Hamburger hypothesized that the development of the nervous system was influenced by signals derived from muscle or organ tissue. He suggested that the signals may influence the division and differentiation of neurons.

With great tenacity, Rita dissected tiny chick embryos, exploring motor neurons in the nervous system jungle. When a motor neuron is stimulated, it instructs muscles to contract which make limbs move. When a limb-bud is amputated, these neurons almost disappear in the spinal cord. Hamburger concluded that the nerve cells diminished and died. But Rita and Levi were able to deduce that these "nerve centers" did start to proliferate, and then died. They were developing the modern concept of nerve cell death as a part of normal development.

As Allied bombing intensified at home, Rita's family fled Turin to a country village. Her lab was now in the corner of the dining room. The Italians overthrew Mussolini and German troops gushed into Italy looking for Jews to admit to their extermination camps. Once again her family fled in desperation to Florence with false identification. At first, research allowed Rita to escape from the horrors of war. It was, she wrote, "a desperate and partially unconscious desire . . . to ignore what is happening in situations where full awareness might lead one to self-destruction." But in the end, the war took all the passion out of research for Rita.

British troops marched through the streets of Florence on November 2, 1944. The war was essentially over. At the start of German occupation, 45,000 Jews existed in Italy; 6,800 did not live to see the war end. Levi-Montalcini volunteered as a doctor with the Allies' health services. Hundreds of refugees, starved by the war, were brought to old military barracks for treatment. An outbreak of Typhoid fever in the barracks stole up to fifty lives a day. Rita knew that working with these patients was deleterious to her own health, but by doing so, she was able to ease the sense of guilt she had for not joining partisan forces during the war.

Rita returned home to Turin in May of 1945, depressed from the stale smell of war that lingered throughout the continent. Her spirits were lifted by a letter from Viktor Hamburger, who had read her articles in Belgian and Swiss journals (she could not publish in Italy at the time because of her heritage). Viktor Hamburger was the man who inspired Rita to explore chick embryos. He invited her to Washington University in St. Louis to further explore the concept of nerve growth factor. She sailed for the U.S. in September of 1946.

As one might imagine, the atmosphere was considerably different at Washington University than fascist Italy. Some classes were even held on the lawns, while barefooted students listened in earnest. Professor Hamburger, a German-born Jew, was in stark contrast to the Professors she had interacted with in Italy. He was soft-spoken, humble, and kind. In her words, he was "a very sophisticated person . . . a very learned, very refined human being."

Hamburger and Levi-Montalcini complemented each other beautifully. He was historically and analytically oriented, and had a strong background in embryology. Rita was bold and intuitive and had a strong background in neurology. They collaborated closely inside and outside of the laboratory, but a healthy sense of competition always existed between them.

In the United States, Rita reveled in the freedom to dedicate her life to her work. She often worked in her laboratory until midnight. There were few distractions from work in St. Louis, save perhaps a Sunday boat cruise on the Mississippi or an elegant dinner party with her Italian-American and scientist friends.

By 1953, Levi-Montalcini and Hamburger published two papers together on nerve cell growth and how macrophages combat dead cells. Rita conducted all of the experiments because Viktor was busy as the chairman of the department, but they were in constant communication about Rita's new discoveries. Hamburger directed Rita to Elmer Bueker, a part-time Ph.D. student, and his research on fast-growing tumor tissues. Bueker had grafted a tumor from a mouse onto a chick embryo and found that the tumor produced the same effect as a developing limb on the nervous system. Rita set out to replicate the experiment and she was astounded at the results.

The bundles of nerve fibers had penetrated the tumor and cut off its blood supply. The same thing happened when she affixed the tumor to a membrane outside of the body, which can only communicate through the circulatory system. She concluded that the tumor must be emitting a substance to make the nerve fibers grow so abundantly.

According to her autobiography, Levi-Montalcini was ecstatic about the results and was desperate to speed up the experimental process. She thought perhaps an old medical school friend might be able to help her do this. Hertha Meyer, who had emigrated to Rio de Janeiro to escape the Nazis, had become an expert in growing tissues in a glass dish (in vitro). When Rita secured a grant to travel to Brazil, she quickly grabbed two tumor-infected mice and jumped on the first plane, smuggling the mice through customs in her overcoat pocket.

In Brazil, Rita attempted to make the nerve cells grow in vitro. She would later write: "[It was] one of the most intense periods of my life, in which moments of enthusiasm and despair alternated with the regularity of a biological clock." On one of her last attempts, she placed part of the mouse tumor next to a bit of nerve tissue in a drop of clotted blood. The results were amazing. Within hours, the tumor had made the nerve fibers grow into a magnificent halo-like form.

Rita returned to St. Louis excited to spend the next several months identifying the nerve growth factor (NGF). Hamburger hired an assistant, a young postdoctoral fellow at Washington University named Stanley Cohen. Another great team was formed. Stanley was a steady and unpretentious biochemist and Rita, always presumptuous and ready to take risks, was an expert in bioembryology. Cohen once told her: "Rita, you and I are good, but together we're wonderful." Instead of a couple of months, they would spend the next six years trying to identify the nerve growth factor.

Levi-Montalcini and Cohen finally identified the compound in a solution of proteins and acids, but they were not sure which one was the active ingredient. Arthur Kornberg, an enzyme biochemist who later won a Nobel Prize, suggested they use snake venom to test the nerve tissue because snake venom held enzymes that would break down nucleic acids but leave the protein untouched. The venom produced a beautiful halo with three thousand times more growth factor than mouse tumors. They knew that the salivary gland was the mammalian equivalent of the venom producing snake gland and thus concluded that the salivary gland of a male mouse must have an enormous amount of growth factor.

With Hamburger's recommendation, Levi-Montalcini was promoted to full professor in 1958. But Cohen was unfortunately forced to leave in 1959 as the department could no longer afford to keep on a biochemist in the zoology department. Rita was heartbroken. The years with Cohen she wrote, "were the most intense and productive years of my life." She consequently abandoned the NGF project.

In 1961, Rita founded a research unit in Rome. Soon she was spending half the year in Italy and half the year in the States. This arrangement seemed to cure her homesickness. Securing grants from the Italian government, however, was a difficult task given the country's bureaucracy. At times, her researchers were not paid for months, but stayed out of loyalty to Levi-Montalcini. The Laboratory of Cell Biology would nevertheless become one of the largest biological research centers in Italy.

Soon Rita realized that she could not give up on her research on the nerve growth factor; she had become too intensely involved with the experiment to simply walk away. She was also annoyed that other scientists were repeating her experiments without mentioning how NGF was discovered. She wrote later: "My name was entirely left out of the literature . . . I am not a person to be bitter, but it was astonishing to find it completely canceled." She was, however, elected to the prestigious National Academy of Sciences in 1968.

Levi-Montalcini conducted further research with Piero Angeletti, with whom she published a classic review article. In 1972, Ruth Hogue Angeletti, Rita's postdoctoral fellow, and Ralph Bradshaw, a young biochemist at the University, identified the exact sequence of the nerve growth factor's amino acids. Finally, the existence of nerve growth factor was veritable.

Rita spent the next several years vigorously promoting the discovery of NGF. She lectured around the world, attempting to spark the scientific community's interest in NGF. Passionate about "her baby," her lectures were famous for extending far beyond the designated time frame.

Rita even adopted a new look to sell NGF. Back in medical school, Rita admitted to wearing "nunnish" outfits. Her image matured considerably since her graduate school days. She designed a basic high necked sleeveless dress and matching jacket, and had several ensembles made in Italy in silk and brocade. She accented her new outfit with four-inch heels, pearls, and an antique broach. This is how Rita arrived to work everyday.

The importance of NGF was obvious and the Nobel committee took note. Rita Levi-Montalcini and Stanley Cohen were awarded the Nobel Prize for Medicine and Physiology in 1986. The honor was especially rewarding after almost 50 years of exploring the concept of nerve growth.

It was never disputed that Levi-Montalcini deserved the Nobel Prize for her discovery, but there were many in the scientific community who believed Viktor Hamburger should have received the Nobel Prize as well. As neuroscientists Dale Purves and Joshua Sanes wrote for *Trends in Neuroscience* in 1987: "Hamburger set the stage in the 1920s, 1930s, and 1940s . . . His exclusion tends to obscure a line of research that now spans more than fifty years."

Although the Nobel Prize is only given for discoveries and not for a lifetime of achievement, Rita felt compelled to defend her discovery and the committee's decision. In an interview with *Omni* magazine she proclaimed: "I've been on excellent terms with Viktor Hamburger . . . He has been an excellent chairman of the department. He was very gentle with me — never any disaffection, despite the fact that the Nobel came to me and not to him. But I believe this is correct. Viktor is a very learned person who's always done excellent work. But he never discovered NGF." Some, like Dale Purves, believed she slighted the contributions of Viktor Hamburger. Indeed, Rita's relationship with Viktor did not survive the controversy.

Growth factors — the molecules that influence the development of immature cells — did not receive much attention until the mid-1980s. Today, research on NGF continues in laboratories around the world. We now know that NGF prevents cells from dying in their early embryonic stages and may play a crucial role in certain degenerative diseases of the central nervous system. NGF also appears to link the immune system with the nervous system. EGF — Epidermal Growth Factor — is used to heal skin transplants on burn patients. Rita never dreamed NGF would have so many important medical applications.

Rita Levi-Montalcini left lasting impressions on her laboratory colleagues. Her palpable sense of passion and curiosity affected everyone who came into contact with "La Regina" — the Queen, as a friend called her. She was an aristocratic, elegant woman who lived her life with intensity and zest. At times, she could be flamboyant, tempestuous, even irascible. Rita was certainly competitive with her peers and especially obstinate when it came to NGF. Ralph Bradshaw, the young biochemist who helped identify NGF's amino acids, observed: "Rita was extremely possessive of NGF. She viewed it as her private property. It became her child . . . There's almost no one in NGF at one time or another who hasn't been at odds with her." Robert Provine, a postdoctoral fellow at Washington University, described her impetuous disposition as the "Levi-Montalcini Roller Coaster."

Rita could also be very giving and kind. She helped the daughter of a tyrannical Italian professor and her fiancé immigrate to the United States so that they could get married. Undergraduate students at Washington University remember Rita as encouraging and supportive. And she never stopped sending CARE packages to her family in Italy.

In her eighties, Rita moved in with her beloved twin, Paola, in Rome and continued to follow a rigorous schedule. The Nobel Prize made her a national heroine and quite a celebrity. According to a local joke, the Pope is easily recognized — provided he appeared with Rita Levi-Montalcini. She used her celebrity status to promote science in Italy and around the world. Her last years were booked with countless meetings — meetings with Italian-American politicians, and with Parliament to discuss tax plans and the effects on science — and as the full-time director at The Laboratory of Cell Biology. She kept her chauffeur and her two secretaries constantly busy.

Although Rita still directed several wide-ranged research projects, in her later years she focused her efforts on NGF and degenerative diseases of the nervous system, such as Multiple Sclerosis. She once declared: "The moment you stop working, you are dead . . . For me, it would be unhappiness beyond anything else." Before Rita Levi-Montalcini stopped working on April 23, 1995, she had untangled the complexities of the nervous system and forever changed our knowledge of healing through the magic lenses of her microscope.

Chapter 15

ℬ⊃ℭ

Rosalind E. Franklin

She stomped her foot down in protest. Her father would not allow it. "Rosalind," he said, "women should get married and do volunteer work . . . and the only women that work are ones that *have* to work." But Rosalind Franklin wanted nothing more than to become a scientist.

Rosalind was born the second of five children on July 25, 1920, in London, to a British-Jewish family of considerable wealth. Her father, Ellis Franklin, was a successful banker who volunteered at the Working Men's College and helped numerous Jews escape from Nazi Germany. Muriel Waley, Rosalind's mother, also dedicated her time to public service. Rosalind was brought up in an intellectual family committed to benevolent causes.

Despite the tenacious and resolute women that surrounded Rosalind while she was growing up, she always felt that there were disadvantages to being a girl; indeed, she felt discriminated against. Instead of nurturing her analytical mind, her parents encouraged her to play with dolls. Rosalind hated dolls.

At a very young age, Rosalind demonstrated her impatience with unsubstantiated speculation and shoddy arguments. Absurdities annoyed her. Rosalind put her faith in facts. She read through the Bible to find

Source: King's College London

out if God existed. She was not impressed with the evidence and questioned: "Well, anyhow, how do you know He isn't a She?"

At St. Paul's Girls' School, her inquisitive mind led her to the field of science. She spent countless hours following star maps in the *London Times* and searching the dark skies for constellations. She excelled in Chemistry, Physics, and French, and at age fifteen, she decided to become a scientist.

To no one's surprise, Rosalind passed the Cambridge University entrance examinations. Her traditional minded father, however, refused to contribute a dime to his daughter's "silly" ambition. Rosalind all but gave up on her dream to become a physical chemist, when Alice Franklin, her aunt, informed Rosalind's father that she would pay for a Cambridge education if he would not. Her mother joined in and also offered to support Rosalind's academic endeavors. Rosalind's father was overpowered, and gave in. Her father's lack of encouragement only strengthened Rosalind's unyielding desire and commitment to her chosen vocation.

In 1938, Rosalind Franklin registered at Newnham College, the women's college at Cambridge University. It was not an easy time, as World War II erupted a year later. Her father implored her to give up her studies and contribute full-time to volunteer defense work. Rosalind had her own ideas about contributing to the war effort. After a brief stint conducting research with future Nobel Prize winning chemist Ronald Norrish, Rosalind began studying the physical structure of coals and carbon for the British Coal Utilization Research Association. She set out to unearth a more efficient way for her country to use coals and charcoal.

Rosalind soon uncovered that when coal and carbons are heated, they undergo certain structural changes. Some heated carbons develop into graphite as their molecules form parallel layers that slip and slide apart. She published five papers in three years on the subject that are still quoted today. The papers proved to be extremely important not only for the charcoal industry, but also for the field of nuclear power. For this achievement, she earned a doctorate from Cambridge University in 1945. At age 26, Rosalind Franklin had established herself as an expert in industrial chemistry.

Rosalind continued to study crystallography, a technique used to reveal the position of atoms within matter. Crystallography involves the "basic experimental technique of X-ray diffraction [which] consists of mounting a sample in the path of a beam (usually an X-ray or neutron beam), recording the positions and intensities of the diffracted beams, and using this information to determine the molecular structure of the material under consideration." Rosalind chose to study the more complex, disordered crystals like carbon and large biological molecules.

After the war, Rosalind contacted Adrienne Weil, an old friend from Cambridge and a French physicist who worked with the Curies at the Radium Institute. Weil found Rosalind a job in Paris as a "chercheur" at the Laboratoire Central des Services Chimiques de l'Etat studying graphitizing and nongraphitizing carbons using X-ray diffraction techniques. There she would spend the happiest three years of her life.

Rosalind felt a refreshing sense of independence and freedom in France. At Cambridge, the men and women did not socialize in the laboratory and were not even permitted to eat together. The atmosphere in Paris was much more casual than Cambridge. Rosalind loved it and, according to her closest friends, before long, she shed her British reserve. It revealed an innocent side to her. She took great delight in joining her co-workers for picnics in the mountains, dinners in bistros, and camping and skiing trips. She frequently arranged 20-mile hiking tours in the mountains, rain or shine. Rosalind enjoyed the comradeship she shared with her male colleagues, especially that of Vittorio Luzzati, her "copain" inside and outside the lab.

Most of her colleagues were young Communists from the French Resistance. For the first time she saw the world outside of her own sheltered, protected home through the eyes of others. Rejecting her parents' well-to-do lifestyle, Rosalind became a Socialist.

With mixed feelings, she returned home to England in 1950 to join John Randell's team of physicists, chemists, and biologists studying living cells at King's College at the University of London. Rosalind knew the crystallographic frontier revolved around biological substances, and thus she accepted Randell's three-year Turner-Newall Research Fellowship. This is where the trouble began.

Randell promised Rosalind she would be working on a new topic alone, except for a few graduate students. Rosalind and her assistant, Raymond Gosling, began exploring the structure of certain biological fibers, namely DNA (deoxyribonucleic acid). Randell's second in command, Maurice Wilkins, apparently was on a short vacation when Rosalind took over the lab. Wilkins expected everyone in the lab to work collectively on one problem, as usual. But this is not how Rosalind operated.

Rosalind, although lighthearted and fun outside of the lab, was private, serious, and intense when in the laboratory. She was as opinionated, stubborn, and hotheaded as the other females in the Franklin family. Not one for idle chit-chat, she loved debates, especially if they were scientific in nature. She was quick, impulsive, passionate, and decisive. She said what she wanted to, when she wanted to. The passive and reserved Wilkins later confided to a friend, "she scared the wits out of me."

Franklin and Gosling continued to work together attempting to decipher the molecular structure of DNA. With the experience she had gained from working with coals and carbon, she knew how to work with materials that were not fully crystalline. She was able to uncover a more competent method of aligning DNA's thin fibers. By adjusting the humidity to which the fibers were exposed, Rosalind discovered that the DNA molecule had two forms: a dry A-form and a wet B-form. She was also able to deduce the location of the phosphate sugars in DNA because the molecule could easily absorb and give off water from the air around it. According to her own notes, Rosalind concluded that the molecule was "a helical structure (which must be very closely packed) containing probably 2, 3, or 4 co-axial nucleic chains per helical unit, and having the phosphate groups near the outside." She also resolved that the bases were inside, away from the water, and ascended up the staircase-like structure. At that point, Rosalind Franklin was just three steps away from explaining heredity.

Other scientists came to hear Rosalind lecture on the subject of DNA at King's College. James Watson and Francis Crick unsuccessfully attempted to produce a model of the DNA molecule from the information provided by Franklin's lecture. Watson's recollection of the water content of Rosalind's DNA samples was clearly wrong. Rosalind Franklin was not shy about pointing out their miscalculations. Watson later admitted, "[m]ost annoying, her objections were not mere perversity." Thus, by the spring of 1952, Rosalind was still the only full-time DNA researcher making significant progress.

After 62 hours of exposure, Rosalind succeeded in taking one of the most beautiful, detailed photographs of DNA. The picture is still unrivaled today. It was clear that the photographed cruciform pattern originated from the helix-shaped molecule. But, after weeks of trying to solve intricate mathematical calculations (no one had ever used the Patterson calculations to solve a fiber structure), Rosalind began to doubt whether the other DNA form, the dry A-form of DNA, was also helical.

All of Rosalind's primary research and calculations were done alone. Although she enjoyed working alone, doing things *her* way, she soon realized that in the laboratory, it was crucial to have a collaborator. She had missed the chance to work with Linus Pauling, a brilliant American chemist, because the U.S. State Department refused to issue him a passport, alleging that he was a Communist (Pauling always denied the charge). Wilkins was a candidate, but Rosalind could not tolerate him. Francis Crick may have been a suitable research partner, but Rosalind found him to be a peculiar theoretician who had wild ideas based on suppositions. Crick later wrote: "I'm afraid we always used to adopt — let's say, a patronizing attitude towards her."

In 1953, Wilkins apparently pulled Franklin's photograph of the B-form of DNA from her desk drawer, without her permission or her knowledge. He secretly showed Watson the photograph, which highlighted the helix structure and its exact conformational relationships. They had not succeeded in making a comparable photograph of DNA. Crystallographer David Harker would later comment that "these people are outside scientific morals, as I know them." In an interview with Anne Sayre, Wilkins addressed the issue: "Perhaps I should have asked Rosalind's permission and I didn't. Things were very difficult. Some people have said that I was entirely wrong to do this without her permission, without consulting her at least, and perhaps I was." In any case, the competitive and cutthroat race to discover the exact structure of DNA had started long before, but after Rosalind's picture was exposed, it was nearing the finish.

Watson and Crick also obtained a government report written by Franklin that same year. The report had been prepared for the Biophysics Committee of the British Medical Research Council, which King's College hosted. Max Perutz, a young chemist from Cavendish Laboratories at Cambridge, attended the meeting and later wrote in *Science* magazine:

> As far as I can remember, Crick heard about the existence of the report from Wilkins, with whom he had frequent contact, and either he or Watson asked me if they could see it. I realized later that, as a matter of courtesy, I should have asked Randell for permission to show it to Watson and Crick, but in 1953 I was inexperienced and casual in administrative matters and since the report was not confidential, I saw no reason for withholding it.

The report led Watson and Crick to the conclusion that the elements under study resembled horse hemoglobin crystals. Crick was also able to deduce that one of the outside chains of the DNA molecule must go up and the other down. Franklin's red exercise book later revealed that she too had been drawing figure eights, but she was a step behind Crick and Watson at that point. Aaron Klug, who would later collaborate with Franklin, noted: "Oh, it's awful. I can't bear to look at [her exercise book]. She's finally making the right connections between A and B. She's shuttling back and forth between the two things . . . it is rather heartbreaking to look at these notebooks and see how close she had come to the solution herself."

Using evidence found by biochemist Erwin Chargaff, Watson and Crick put the final pieces of the puzzle together. Each step of the helical staircase consisted of pairs of bases, a *particular* pair of bases. This is how genetic information is passed from generation to generation. Watson and Crick told everyone of their discovery except Franklin and Wilkins.

On March 17, 1953, Rosalind submitted a paper to *Nature* magazine, outlining what she had uncovered from the spectacular B-form photograph. Just eleven days earlier, Watson and Crick had submitted an article unlocking the DNA mystery. Rosalind had lost the race.

Watson and Crick's article was but one page. They thanked physical chemist Jerry Donohue for his constant advice and criticism, and in the second to the last sentence they added: "We have been stimulated by a knowledge of the general nature of the unpublished experimental results and ideas of Dr. M. H. F. Wilkins, Dr. R. E. Franklin, and their co-workers at King's College, London." Rosalind would never learn that their double helix model was based on *her* experimental evidence.

Not surprisingly, Rosalind left Kings College soon after Watson and Crick's article was published. She joined John Desmond Bernal's research team at Birbeck College, the graduate night school of the University of London. She was permitted to keep the fellowship from King's College as long as she gave up her prior work on nucleic acids. At Birbeck she headed her own research group, which consisted of two graduate students, Kenneth Holmes and John Finch, along with Aaron Klug, who became her only collaborator, and won the Nobel Prize for chemistry in 1982. Over the next five years, she became the world's leading expert in helical structures.

Rosalind's team focused on ribonucleic acid (RNA). In studying the structure of RNA, the group hoped to unveil how a virus particle can grow and produce other cells. They were able to do this with several RNA-containing viruses. Rosalind relied on the tobacco mosaic virus (TMV) to aid in their understanding of the organization of other regular virus particles. She determined that RNA exists, not in the helix's central cavity as suspected, but in the subunits of the virus's protein coat. This made it possible to understand the structural relationship between protein and a nucleic acid and how they fit together. They were laying the foundations of structural virology. Rosalind published over seventeen articles on viruses. Her colleagues considered her to be one of the "major founders of biomolecular science." Bernal later wrote: "At the same time she proved to be an admirable director of a research team and inspired those who worked with her to reach the same high standard."

Franklin's success led to numerous conferences around the world. In 1956, she lectured in London, Madrid, and the United States. She spent time in New Haven, St. Louis, Los Angeles, and Berkeley, where she worked with Nobel Prize winner Wendell Stanley. It was late that summer that she suffered from episodes of excruciating pain.

Rosalind was diagnosed with ovarian cancer at the age of thirty-six. Over the next two years, she underwent three operations and experimental chembtherapy. She did not talk to anybody about it except her family and research group. With the cancer in remission, Rosalind returned to her active life, which included mountain climbing, tennis, and, of course, hours and hours in the laboratory.

Rosalind and her research team had moved to the MCR Laboratory of Molecular Biology to Cambridge, when Frederick Schaffer's laboratory at the University of California at Berkeley stumbled upon some crystallized polio virus. They sent the crystals to Franklin's team for analysis as soon as possible. The precariousness of working with an infectious virus was offset, sadly, by Franklin's knowledge of her own cancer.

Rosalind was thrilled to be asked to exhibit two models of virus molecules for the 1957 Brussels World Fair. Franklin, Holmes, Finch, and Klug put together a six-foot-tall TMV virus molecule model with dozens of white plastic oval pieces. The Royal Institute of Great Britain proudly displayed the model before it was shipped to Brussels where 42 million visitors got their first look at what makes up all living things.

The day after organizing a dinner party for her parents' 40th wedding anniversary, Rosalind checked into a hospital, knowing that she would never leave. She died on April 16, 1958, just minutes before her last paper was to be read at the Faraday Society.

Watson, Crick, and Wilkins won the Nobel Prize for medicine for their work on DNA four years after Rosalind Franklin's death. Watson and Crick's Nobel lecture cited 98 references and not one of the references recognized Rosalind's extensive research on the subject. Wilkins was the only winner to include her in his acknowledgments.

Could Watson, Crick, and Wilkins have uncovered the DNA mystery and received a Nobel Prize had they not obtained experimental data surreptitiously from Rosalind Franklin? Would Rosalind have won the Nobel Prize had she lived? Many still argue that if Rosalind had lived, she would have received the Nobel Prize for her contributions. In 1989, Anthony Serafini's biography of Linus Pauling commented: "There are so many actual and possible degrees of unethical behavior that it is difficult to draw the line. Sometimes, of course, the case is clear, as when James Watson made use of Rosalind Franklin's data without crediting her in the famed DNA race . . . Certainly Watson and Crick would not have gotten the Nobel Prize had they not stolen her data."

Watson wrote the renowned book, *The Double Helix,* six years later about the discovery of DNA. In his book he would confirm a statement he had made years before about his role in DNA: "Except for my writing, all my work has been getting other people to help me. If I have to use someone else to get the answer, I'll do it . . . The most important thing in science is getting the answer, not showing that you've done it yourself . . . It helps you doing science if you're very social." He achieved "success" from his book, which was widely read, but his admission that he had used Rosalind's notes without her permission corroded his scientific contributions. His admission may have given Rosalind the scientific credit she deserved, but as Anne Sayre claimed: "He carelessly robbed Rosalind of her personality."

"Rosy" is Watson's central rival in *The Double Helix.* Watson was uninhibited in portraying "Rosy" (nobody called her Rosy) as an unattractive, dowdy, rigid old maid. He described her as overly obstinate and deliberate. He even ridiculed her scientific ability, accusing her of being "anti-helical" and opposed to model building.

Elizabeth Janeway commented on Watson's book in *Man's World, Woman's Place*: "We may, however, take advantage of his candor to note Watson's idea of where women belong in science: outside of it." Robert Sinsheimer claimed the book is "unbelievably mean in spirit, filled with the distorted and cruel perceptions of childish insecurity." What made *The Double Helix* even more heartless was Franklin's inability to defend herself against anyone's misrepresentations. Many of her colleagues and closest friends were outraged at Watson's distortions of her character and quickly came to her defense. Anne Sayre, a long-time friend of Franklin, wrote *Rosalind Franklin and DNA* to counteract Watson's "Personal Account of the Discovery of the Structure of DNA." And Aaron Klug, one of Rosalind's biggest supporters and only collaborator, in an attempt to repair Rosalind's reputation, carefully outlined her DNA contributions for *Nature* magazine in two papers.

Sayre recalls Rosalind as a strikingly handsome woman who did not resemble the badly dressed, bluestocking character of "Rosy." Additionally, the people who had the privilege of knowing Rosalind outside of the laboratory, remember her as warm, kind, and humorous. Words like "lighthearted," and even "prankish" were used to describe Rosalind. She sewed brightly colored patches over the pockets of her lab coats because she felt they were too dreary. Rosalind certainly had many admirers who embraced and cherished her generous and colorful personality. One of her graduate students, Kenneth Holmes, said: "[Rosalind] had charisma. She was a fascinating, very attractive woman, and she affected all of us in a very deep way. Her friends and students have great difficulty thinking about her because it's so painful."

Although many agree Watson's rendition of the DNA race distorted Rosalind's character, few, even Anne Sayre, would disagree that there was a "difficult" side to her. Rosalind's mother once wrote:

> Rosalind felt passionately about many things, and on occasion could be tempestuous. Her affections both in childhood, and in later life, were deep and strong and lasting, but she could never be demonstrative, or readily express her feelings in words. This combination of strong feeling, sensibility and emotional reserve, often complicated by intense concentration on the matter of the moment . . . could provoke either stony silence or a storm . . . the strong will and a certain imperiousness and tempestuousness of temper, remained characteristic all her life.

Her thesis advisors at Cambridge evidently found Rosalind to be stubborn and difficult to work with. Certainly, many researchers who worked with her in the laboratory would confirm that she was not easy to collaborate with. Raymond Gosling said: "She didn't suffer fools gladly at all. You either had to be on the ball, or you were lost in any discussion about anything, and that was constant." Donald Casper, who worked on viruses with Rosalind, has said: "She wouldn't put up with nonsense.

She was a very vital human being who didn't indulge in speculation." Aaron Klug recalled: "She could be very pleasant, and she had a sense of fun. But in the lab, she was actually quite tough. She could snap at people . . . It would have gone quite unremarked if she had been a man. But she stood up for things . . . [and] was rather persistent." Rosalind was rigorously committed to science and did not fancy anyone who did not display the same serious dedication in the laboratory.

Rosalind was indeed passionate about science; her devotion was of great intensity. She made a conscious decision to sacrifice both marriage and children for her scientific curiosity. As Sayre writes: "Rosalind possessed a fierce but happy sense of vocation."

One thing about Rosalind Franklin remains largely undisputed — her scientific contributions were numerous and brilliant. She made pivotal contributions to the study of coal, DNA, and plant viruses. Awards for Rosalind were few, but as Sayre writes: "That they were approaching when she died is beyond doubt." Reporting her death, *The New York Times* applauded Rosalind as one of "a select band of pioneers" — a pioneer who made the discovery of DNA, the source of genetic inheritance for all living things, possible.

Chapter 16

ഇ)ര

Dorothy Crowfoot Hodgkin

By the time she died in 1994, the famed scientist and Oxford professor Dorothy Crowfoot Hodgkin had traveled to some of the world's most exotic locations. It was often to conduct scientific research, give a lecture, participate in an international committee, or receive an award. But perhaps even more often, the international travel was to see her parents who, due to their jobs, were often abroad since Dorothy was a child. Later, Dorothy continued her international journeys to spend some time with her husband, whose job also required extensive travel. Dorothy's three children each demonstrated a similar penchant for travel, as they flew to Stockholm from New Delhi, Zambia, and Algeria to witness their mother become the third female recipient of the Nobel Prize for Chemistry.

Dorothy Crowfoot Hodgkin is not generally known, however, for her international travel. Rather, she is most noted for her life-long scientific journey, one that required persistence, courage, intelligence, intuition, and imagination. It was a journey not to far-off places, but deep into the inner structure of the atoms and molecules that create what is sometimes referred to as the "flowers of the mineral kingdom." Indeed, Dorothy spent most of her life on a journey to the inside of the crystal.

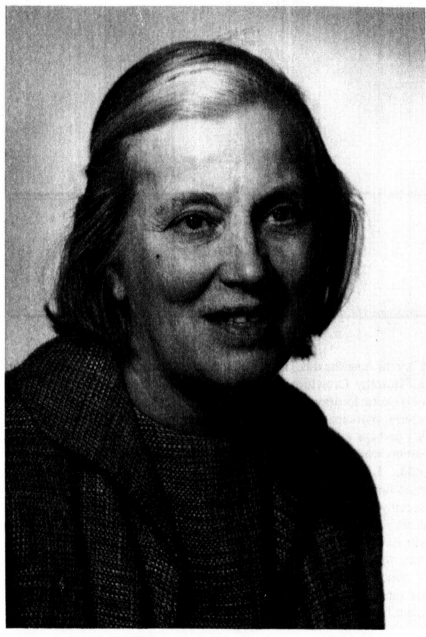

Source: AIP Emilio Segrè Visual Archives,
          Physics Today Collection

Grace Crowfoot gave birth to Dorothy on May 12, 1910, in Cairo. Dorothy's comfort with foreign soil probably began shortly thereafter, as she spent the first four years of her life as a young English girl growing up in Egypt. At the time, Cairo was under English rule. Her father, John Winter Crowfoot, was a scholar in both the classics and archaeology and worked as an inspector for England's Ministry of Education in the Egyptian Education Service in Cairo. Grace was a self-taught amateur botanist and later became an authority on Coptic textiles. In 1914, her father was offered the position of Director of Education and Antiquities and Principal of Gordon College in Khartoum. The first World War, however, caused the Crowfoots to fear an invasion of Egypt by Turkish troops. When Dorothy was only four, John and Grace Crowfoot gathered up their girls and sent them on a boat to England for safekeeping where they were watched over by a nanny and their paternal grandmother. Dorothy and her two younger sisters were separated from their mother for three years.

In 1918, Grace returned to England, bringing along with her Dorothy's new baby sister. Feeling the need to reacquaint herself with her daughters, Grace rounded up the girls and created a new home for them in Lincoln, England. Here, Grace began to home-school her children, teaching them history, literature, and natural science.

The education Dorothy and her sisters received from their mother was unusual. Their mother made the girls write their own history books under her guidance, including the different reigns of the kings of England, and what people wore and what homes they lived in, and the poetry they wrote. Through techniques like this, Grace helped her daughters develop their imagination and creative thinking skills while they learned a subject or tackled an academic problem.

After World War II, the "widely dispersed" family Dorothy had begun to know continued in a regular pattern. Every summer, her father and mother would travel to England and live with their children. After three months, Dorothy's father would return to his job overseas and after six months, Dorothy's mother would join him. Dorothy would occasionally visit her parents during her childhood, traveling to such places as Sudan and Palestine. During these years, Dorothy began to show an interest in academic and scientific pursuits. Before beginning her formal scholastic training at the Sir John Leman School, the budding young scientist was able to attend a small private class where she performed some elementary chemistry. One of her experiments resulted in the growth of crystals. Dorothy found the geometrical shapes contained in the structure of the crystal both elegant and beautiful. Could it someday be possible to discover the structural design that produced these geometrical shapes? Is it likely that someday we will possibly discover how nature produces such elegance and beauty? From these days in her youth until the day she died, Dorothy was enchanted by the mysteries inherent in the crystal.

Dorothy's parents, both of whom were academically-inclined, greatly supported and encouraged Dorothy's wish to investigate nature's mysteries through the sciences. At the age of eleven, Dorothy entered the Sir John Leman School and quickly began focusing her efforts on learning the history of crystallography and chemistry, a subject that was generally reserved for boys.

Her thirst for knowledge about the crystal gained momentum when, in 1923, at the age of thirteen, she and her sister Joan visited their father in Khartoum. John Crowfoot, who was now a member of the Governor General's Council, had just been appointed Director of Education and Antiquities for the Sudan. While in Khartoum, Dorothy began to discover that the academic background of her parents was surely to her advantage. Here, she was able to meet one of her father's good friends, A. F. Joseph, who would later be referred to as "Uncle Joe." Uncle Joe took a great liking to Dorothy and a great interest in her potential career as a scientist. A. F. Joseph was a soil chemist and worked in the Welcome Laboratory in Khartoum. To entertain their young visitors, Uncle Joe and the other scientists gave the girls tours of the laboratory and taught them how to pan for gold. "Uncle Joe" was Dorothy's first mentor. Before leaving Khartoum, Uncle Joe gave Dorothy a unique going away present — a box of minerals that enabled Dorothy to create her first home-laboratory upon returning to England.

Two years after this experience, Grace introduced her daughter Dorothy to a book that would indirectly shape the rest of her life, entitled *Concerning the Nature of Things*. It was written by W. H. Bragg and contained information concerning a relatively new scientific technique called X-ray crystallography.

W. H. Bragg, and the younger W.L. Bragg, together with Max van Laue, were the founding fathers of this new scientific breakthrough. X-ray crystallography is similar to photography. Photography's Latin definition is "writing with light" (graphy = writing, photo = light). The magic of photography is that a camera can "write" a picture if light is "shot" through it and captured on a photographic surface. X-ray crystallography is another type of "writing," which occurs when an X-ray is shot through a crystal and is captured on a photographic plate.

Max van Laue first discovered that when an X-ray is shot through a crystal, the x-ray can be diffracted and the "writing" is captured on a photographic plate. Sometimes the X-rays would interfere with each other and cancel out any writing that would have resulted, but Laue learned that if deflected X-rays constructively interacted with each other, a bright spot could be captured on the photographic plate. The writing that resulted on the photographic plate appeared as if X-ray crystallography was in reality, just a bunch of spots. Laue also discovered, however, that the patterns these spots created were not random. These spots were actually a type of code that explained the structure of a particular crystal. Each crystal had its own particular code that could be analyzed through a series of complex mathematical formulas and calculations. If a scientist could correctly crack the code, they could discover vital information regarding the structure of the atoms and molecules of a crystal. This was significant progress in the sciences because, since atoms and molecules are the primary building blocks of all matter, once the precise mathematical formula of the structure of a particular substance was understood, the ability to create that substance would be possible.

Through X-ray crystallography, scientists were now able to determine the size, shape, and positions of these atoms and molecules. Essentially, this new technique allowed scientists to determine the molecular structure of almost any crystal or crystalline material. The more complicated the structure inside a crystal, however, the more elaborate, complicated, and arduous were the mathematical calculations necessary to determine a crystal's true structure.

Initially, this meant that X-ray crystallography had very few practical applications. The organic chemists of the day, who were trained in determining molecular structures through traditional methods, regarded crystallography as a "black art." Whether X-ray crystallography had practical scientific applications did not matter to Dorothy. She was fascinated with the findings of Braggs and Laue when they wrote: "Broadly speaking, the discovery of X-rays has increased the keenness of our vision over ten thousand times and we can now 'see' the individual atoms and molecules." Little did Dorothy know that she would one day become an expert in the field of X-ray crystallography, and that W.H. Bragg himself would publicly claim that her discoveries were so monumental to be equated with "breaking the sound barrier."

Curiously, not too long after reading *Concerning the Nature of Things*, Dorothy questioned her future in science. Her father was offered a more prestigious academic post as director of the British School of Archaeology in Jerusalem and two years later, when Dorothy graduated from the Sir John Leman School at age 18, she moved to Jerusalem to be close to her parents. They were by this time her biggest academic role models, and Dorothy soon became a functioning member of an archaeological crew whose primary purpose was to excavate ancient Byzantine churches. At this time Dorothy began seriously entertaining the idea of becoming an archeologist. Although Dorothy found much intellectual and emotional satisfaction from being a part of this important scientific and historical endeavor, her love of the crystal and of chemistry in general led her back to English soil. After many long hours of intensive study, Dorothy successfully passed the entrance examinations and was accepted by Somerville College in Oxford to formally continue her studies in Chemistry.

At Somerville College, Dorothy began a friendship with the principal of the college, Margery Fry. Margery had devoted much of her time campaigning against the death penalty and for penal reform. Similarly, Dorothy's humanitarian interests had been cultivated early by her mother Grace, who had lost four of her own brothers to war. She would take young Dorothy to league meetings in Geneva designed to help eradicate war and cultivate peace.

Dorothy also began to find opportunities for herself in the field of chemistry at Somerville. Because her parents were abroad, Dorothy stayed at college through the summer and found work in the university laboratories. Eventually, the noted scientist E. G. J. Hartley lent Dorothy the keys to his laboratory. Soon after, Dorothy was employed by H. M. Powell as his first research assistant in his laboratory. Together they began working with X-ray crystallography, a serious discipline that required a keen mind, persistence, and patience. Her poise and enthusiasm helped her to excel in this demanding science, and she developed a keen interest in a particular type of crystal known as sterols. Dorothy's graduation from Somerville College in 1932, however, left her unsure about which step to take next.

Luckily, that same year, "Uncle Joe" was in England. While on board a local train, Uncle Joe met one of Cambridge University's professors of physical chemistry who had just hired John D. Bernal to be a lecturer at Cambridge. While at Cambridge, Bernal would begin studying sterols. Uncle Joe was able to convince the Cambridge professor to make arrangements for Dorothy to work with Bernal at Cambridge. Then Uncle Joe, the man who taught Dorothy how to pan for gold, convinced her to follow her dreams at Cambridge and study under Bernal.

J. D. Bernal was one of the world's most noted physicists at the time. His research was of particular interest to Dorothy, as it included the study of sterol crystals through X-rays. His laboratory was well financed; and Dorothy, under his guidance, was able to indulge in the study of crystallography fully. Working with Bernal was a watershed event in Dorothy's life. She would later state: "There is a sense in which all of my subsequent work started from looking at crystals with Bernal."

While working with Bernal, Dorothy performed her first series of calculations to determine a molecular structure. Together they worked on the protein crystal, pepsin. While working on the mathematical calculations to crack the code of pepsin, Dorothy helped make significant scientific discoveries. First, she discovered that protein crystals, like pepsin, should be studied while surrounded by their "mother liquid." Conventional scientists had believed that crystals should be dried and then researched. Second, Dorothy helped discover a new use for X-ray crystallography. She learned that X-ray crystallography aided in determining molecular shape, a concept that is key to understanding how molecules affect biological activity. After two years of research and study with Bernal, Dorothy was forced to make the difficult decision to leave Bernal and his team, an important atmosphere of intellectual camaraderie and scientific support for Dorothy. After her scholarships and grants expired, Dorothy was forced to find a way to make a living for herself. Although jobs were scarce in Cambridge, Dorothy was offered the position of Official Fellow and tutor in natural science at her alma mater, Somerville College. There, she taught chemistry at the women's college in the Department of Mineralogy and Crystallography.

Dorothy was determined to continue her studies in X-ray crystallography, but she had a difficult time finding the necessary funds for research. X-ray crystallography was still a brand-new field and equipment was costly and hard to come by. In addition, this was a time when women had not yet developed a well-known reputation as scientists. Dorothy would soon change that; but before reshaping the world of science as we now know it, Dorothy would suffer poor working conditions at Somerville College.

Her laboratory at Somerville was primitive, at best. A small grant had allowed her to obtain a few necessary pieces of equipment, but she could only afford one or two research students to assist her. Together they worked in scattered rooms in Somerville's University Museum, oftentimes in the basement. The room that housed her polarizing microscope was particularly daunting. Each time Dorothy needed to peer through her microscope, which was at least several times a day, she was forced to climb a rickety spiral staircase in order to reach the Gothic window high above — the only window that provided sufficient light.

Nevertheless, Dorothy steadfastly continued the research she had begun with Bernal to determine the structure of a sterol crystal. While at Somerville College, Dorothy crystallized and photographed insulin, the second protein to be studied through X-ray crystallography. Dorothy would later report that this was the most exciting day of her life. Blissfully, she roamed the streets of England pondering the delightful results of her work. Might she become the first scientist to discover the structure of a protein? This was the beginning of a research project that would require another 34 years before its completion.

The working conditions at Somerville had become exceptionally difficult for Dorothy, as she had developed a severe case of rheumatoid arthritis. Treatment for her arthritis was unsuccessful and, eventually, Dorothy began to live with crippled hands and feet. Adding another injury, Oxford had officially barred her from attending research meetings of the faculty chemistry club because she was a woman. Nevertheless, Dorothy continued her work on the crystals found in sterols, but this time she focused her energies on one in particular — cholesteryl iodide.

Through her quiet perseverance and extraordinary scientific talent, Dorothy's career began to blossom. She eventually won both the hearts and minds of the Oxford faculty and student body. Dorothy was soon asked to speak at the student's chemistry club meeting and shortly thereafter, members of the faculty would sit in on club meetings to hear Dorothy speak. While teaching at Oxford, Dorothy would eventually mentor a fourth-year undergraduate student named Margaret Roberts, who would later become Margaret Thatcher, Prime Minister of England. Dorothy was awarded a small series of grants through the Rockefeller Foundation, and graduate students in chemistry began requesting that Dorothy be their faculty advisor and do research with them.

In 1937, Dorothy received her doctorate degree after completing a lengthy dissertation on her research on cholesterol iodide. Dorothy had discovered an unprecedented way in which a person could examine and discover pertinent information about a three-dimensional particle, a particle so small that it could not be seen by the human eye, regardless of the microscope. Her work provided essential information on how and why particular chemical compounds work in living organisms. Dorothy earned significant recognition and praise when her doctoral paper was cited by W.H. Bragg, the man who had discovered crystallography, as being an example of a practical method of determining the three-dimensional structure that passed beyond the limits of organic chemistry.

That same year, Dorothy Crowfoot married Margery Fry's cousin, Thomas Hodgkin. Thomas was already an important member of the academic community as a scholar and teacher in African studies. Serious scholarship was common to his family: his father was an historian at Oxford; both his grandfathers were also historians; and he was both descendant and namesake of Thomas Hodgkin, who discovered what was eventually named Hodgkin's disease, a deadly cancer of the body's lymphatic system. During their early married life, Thomas was a school teacher and later served as director of the Institute of African Studies at the University of Ghana. Because Thomas's job required frequent world travel, the couple maintained separate residences until 1945, when Thomas was given a permanent position teaching at Oxford.

Despite the unusual circumstances of their marriage, Dorothy and Thomas found happiness together. Although there were fears that Dorothy's work with X-rays might prevent her from having children, together Dorothy and Thomas had two sons and a daughter. These children followed in their parents' footsteps, each becoming a world traveler and an academic. Four years after her marriage, Dorothy published an article on the structure of cholestryl iodide in three-dimensional detail. At the time, scientists were not attempting to determine three dimensional structures because they were so complex and required so many mathematical calculations; indeed, many scientists believed to do so was impossible.

Although Dorothy was passionate about cracking the code of insulin, she shifted her focus to researching penicillin at the outbreak of World War II. Again, scientists at the time believed that Dorothy was attempting to achieve the impossible. Chemists had already attempted to decode penicillin by studying its chemical make-up. When they heard a young woman was going to study the structure of penicillin through the "black art" of X-ray crystallography, the scientific world was in an uproar. Dorothy maintained her belief that the structure of penicillin was a ring of atoms — three carbon and one nitrogen. The chemists believed that this particular combination was too unstable to occur in the natural world. Upon hearing her theory, one chemist erupted: "If that's the formula of penicillin, I'll give up chemistry and grow mushrooms!"

Penicillin had been discovered only ten years earlier by Alexander Fleming. Later, Ernst Chain developed a method to purify penicillin and it soon became one of the world's most powerful and useful antibiotics. Due to the increasing number of casualties in World War II, soldiers were in dire need of the medicinal properties of penicillin, as the number of bacterial infections contracted during the war was increasing at a rapid rate. The world, however, was at a standstill in terms of mass-producing penicillin because its chemical structure was still unknown.

Dorothy swiftly assembled a team of scientists at Oxford to analyze the properties of penicillin through X-ray crystallization in hopes of finding a way to mass produce nature's antibiotic. Dorothy and her assistant, Barbara Low, a graduate student at Oxford, began the complicated process of discovering the properties of penicillin. Dorothy shot X-rays through all possible angles through penicillin crystals. The resulting patterns of dots on the photographic plates were analyzed, and the patterns were subject to complicated mathematical calculations. Through this painstaking process, Dorothy and her team were able to determine exactly where the key atoms were located in a penicillin crystal. The mass production of penicillin, however, also required determining the configuration of the electrons surrounding the atoms. This required creating another series of maps which plotted electron-density. Luckily, Dorothy was aided by one of the world's first analog computers, an IBM card-punch machine. This was the first time a computer was used in a direct application to solve a biochemical problem. These punch cards helped Dorothy swiftly create all of the electron-density maps and, in 1944, Dorothy had determined the structure of penicillin.

Two years later, Dorothy was promoted to the position of demonstrator and lecturer at Oxford University, and the following year she received the Rockefeller fellowship. By 1949, Dorothy published her findings of the molecular structure of penicillin, which not only proved her original theory correct, but also provided the world with the necessary information for mass-production. To this day, the world has yet to discover a more powerful or widely used antibiotic. Consequently, Dorothy was given a promotion at the college and her struggles with finances had finally come to an end. She would have to wait another ten years, however, before attaining the position of full professor.

After World War II, Dorothy helped found the International Union of Crystallography. Dorothy insisted on including members of the Communist party in the Union, which was somewhat of a political scandal at the time and caused a stir among various Western governments who had just waged a war against the Soviet Union. Dorothy however, was not merely a scientist, she was also a dedicated humanist committed to world peace. She joined several organizations that allowed the participation of scientists from the Soviet Union. These activities led to problems for Dorothy, particularly when requesting entry visas into the United States. But because of her discoveries and worldwide recognition, Dorothy had numerous scientists who were willing to write letters on her behalf whenever she needed assistance entering a foreign country.

One year before her profound discovery of penicillin's molecular structure, Dorothy began to concentrate on her X-ray crystallography techniques and research on the vitamin B-12. To crack the code of B-12, which contains 90 atoms in its molecular structure, each atom needed to be identified in size, shape, and placement. With the assistance of another graduate student, Jenny Glusker, and an American team of crystallographers, led by Kenneth Trueblood; and later also with John White of Princeton University, Dorothy began a new quest.

Trueblood had access to UCLA's state-of-the-art computer equipment, and Dorothy and Kenneth frequently exchanged their scientific results through the mail and by telegraph. Vitamin B-12 aids in the prevention and cure of pernicious anemia, a blood condition that can cause death. But once again, Dorothy was advised not to take on the project, due to the complexities of the problem at hand: B-12 was four times as large as penicillin and its structure was unique. One year after accepting a position as a University Reader at Oxford and after almost ten years of research and calculations, Dorothy and John White eventually discovered and co-published a report on the molecular structure of B-12. W. L. Bragg, who helped begin the technology of X-ray crystallography, would later cite Dorothy's research on B-12 in his book *Fifty Years of X-Ray Diffraction*, as fundamental in finding new horizons in the field. During the same year, Dorothy continued her philanthropic and sometimes politically controversial endeavors when she became an official member of Pugwash, an international organization of scientists who banded together to research the various scientific and social problems inherent in manufacturing weapons whose sole purpose was mass destruction.

The following year, 1958, Dorothy was finally promoted to full professor at Oxford and was given a new laboratory in a modern wing of the chemistry building. One year later, Dorothy was awarded the Wolfson Research Professorship, which she held through 1977. Her greatest scientific recognition, however, came in 1964, when she became the third woman to receive the Nobel Prize for Chemistry (Marie Curie was the first, and Marie's daughter, Irene Joliot-Curie was the second), for her "determination by X-ray techniques of the structures of important biochemical substances." Newspaper headlines of this event read: "Nobel Prize for British Wife" and "Grandmother Wins Nobel Prize."

The Academy, however, knew that Dorothy was much more than a wife or a grandmother. Before awarding Dorothy the Nobel Prize, Gunar Hagg of the Royal Swedish Academy of Sciences gave a speech shedding light on why Dorothy's research demanded world-wide recognition: "Knowledge of a compound is absolutely essential in order to interpret its properties and reactions and to decide how it might be synthesized from simpler compounds . . . The determination of the structure of penicillin has been described as a magnificent start to a new era of crystallography." The Academy also remarked on Dorothy's "exceptional skill, in which chemical knowledge, intuition, imagination and perseverance has been conspicuous." Dorothy, ever the philanthropist, gave the money from the Nobel Prize to found a scholarship and to forward the efforts of world peace and the relief of famine.

One year later, Dorothy received a piece of mail. "There are certain letters which I dread to open," said Dorothy, "and when I saw one from Buckingham Palace I left it sealed, fearing that they wanted to make me Dame Dorothy." The letter, which was from the Queen of England, offered Dorothy the Order of Merit. Dorothy became the second woman in Britain's history to be awarded with Britain's Order of Merit, the first recipient being Florence Nightingale.

Even after receiving some of the highest awards from both England and the world, Dorothy did not stop her scientific investigations. In 1969, after decades of painstaking research, Dorothy finally completed the research she had begun over thirty years ago, one of the most complex investigations of a molecular structure: Zinc insulin. Zinc insulin contains approximately 800 atoms. Cracking this code was further complicated because insulin crystallizes in several different forms, but Dorothy employed several sophisticated techniques to determine the structure.

Between the ages of 50 and 67, Dorothy received several awards and was granted esteemed positions in both the scientific and academic societies. She received 19 honorary degrees from some of the worlds' most prestigious universities, including Cambridge, Harvard, Chicago, and Brown. The Soviet Union presented her with the Lomonosov Gold Medal of the Soviet Academy of Sciences. She became the President of the International Union of Crystallography between 1972 and 1975 and served as the President of the Pugwash conference on science and world affairs between 1975 and 1993, just one year before her death.

Although Dorothy will forever be remembered as the scientist who discovered the intricate structures of insulin, penicillin, and B-12, those close to her remember Dorothy as a warm and caring mother and teacher. By the time she died in 1994, Dorothy had invited over one hundred scientists to work with her in her laboratory. Her family of colleagues and friends came from all over the world: New Zealand, Canada, Holland, China, Japan, Nigeria, Yugoslavia, New Guinea, and countless other regions. At her personal residence, there was an open-door policy, and her frequent visitors included students, colleagues, friends, revolutionaries, refugees, and famous figures from all over the world. Dorothy's life was full of travel and full of love, but her first love was the crystal, and for that she will always be remembered.

Notes

Some of the useful general sources about women in science include:

Abir-Am and Dorina Outram. (1986) *Uneasy Careers and Intimate Lives: Women in Science, 1700-1945*. New Brunswick: Rutgers University Press.

Berstein, Jeremy. (1978) *Experiencing Science*. New York: Basic Books.

Beyerchen, Alan, D. (1977) *Scientists Under Hitler: Politics and the Physics Community*. New Haven: Yale University Press.

Dash, Joan. (1991) *Triumph of Discovery: Women Scientists Who Won the Nobel Prize*. Englewood Cliffs: Julian Messner.

Deegan, Mary Jo, ed. (1991) *Women in Sociology: A Bio-bibliographical Sourcebook*. New York: Greenwood Press.

Creese, Mary, R. (1998) *Ladies in the Laboratory? American and British Women in Science: A Survey of Their Contributions to Research*. Lanham, Maryland: Scarecrow Press.

Farber, Eduard. (1963) *Nobel Prize Winners in Chemistry*. New York: Abelard-Schuman.

Felder, Deborah, G. (1996) *The One Hundred Most Influential Women of All Time: A Ranking Past and Present*. Secaucus, N. J.: Carol Publishing Group.

Gleasner, Diana. (1979) *Breakthrough, Women in Science*. New York: Harcourt Brace Jovanovich.

Grinstein, Louise, S., Carol A. Biermann, and Rose K. Rose. (1997) *Notable Women in the Biological Sciences: A Bibliographic Sourcebook*. Westport, CT: Greenwood Press.

Haber, Louis. (1979) *Women Pioneers of Science*. New York: Harcourt Brace Jovanovich.

Hacker, Carlotta. (1998) *Nobel Prize Winners*. New York: Crabtree Publishing.

Herzenberg, Caroline, L. (1986) *Women Scientist from Antiquity to the Present: An Index*. West Cornwall, CT: Locust Hill Press.

Hume, R. F. (1964) *Great Women of Medicine*. New York: Random House.

Kass-Simon, G. and Patricia Farnes, eds. (1990) *Women in Science*. Bloomington: Indiana University Press.

Kennedy, Rebecca and Michelle. (1990) *Women in the Sciences*. Washington, Library of Congress.

Kirkup, Gill and Laurie Smith Keller, eds. (1992) *Inventing Women: Science, Technology, and Gender*. Cambridge, MA: Polity Press in association with B. Blackwell and the Open University.

Levin, Beatrice, S. (1980) *Women and Medicine*. Metuchen, N.J.: Scarecrow Press, 1980.

Magill, Frank, N. (1991) *The Nobel Prize Winners, Physiology or Medicine*. Pasadena, CA: Salem Press.

McGrayne, Sharon, Bertsch. (1993) *Nobel Prize Women in Science*. New York: Birch Lane Press.

Mozans, H. J. (1991) *Women in Science*. Notre Dame: University of Notre Dame Press.

Noble, Iris. (1979) *Contemporary Women Scientists of America*. New York: Julian Messner.

Opfell, Olga. (1986) *The Lady Laureates*. Metuchen, N.J.: Scarecrow Press.

Ogilvie, Marilyn, B. (1991) *Women in Science; Antiquity through the 19th Century*. London: MIT Press.

Osen, Lynn, M. (1974) *Women in Mathematics*. Cambridge: MIT Press.

Phillips, Patricia. (1990) *The Scientific Lady: A Social History of Women's Scientific Interests, 1520-1918*. London: Weidenfeld & Nicholson.

Pyclor, Helena, M., Nancy G. Slack, and Pnina G. Abir-Am, eds. (1996) *Creative Couples in Sciences*. New Brunswick, N.J.: Rutgers Univeristy Press.

Rossiter, Margaret, W. (1995) *Women Scientists in America; Before Affirmative Action 1940-1972*. Baltimore: Johns Hopkins University Press.

Rossiter, Margaret, W. (1982) *Women Scientists in America; Struggles and Strategies to 1940*. Baltimore: Johns Hopkins University Press.

Shearer, Benjamin and Barbara S. Shearer, eds. (1997) *Notable Women in the Physical Sciences: A Biographical Dictionary*. Westport, CT: Greenwood Press.

Shearer, Benjamin and Barbara S. Shearer, eds. (1996) *Notable Women in the Life Sciences: A Biographical Dictionary*. Westport, CT: Greenwood Press.

Shiels, Barbara. (1985) *Women and the Nobel Prize*. Minneapolis, Dillon Press.

Siegal, Patricia, Joan. (1985) *Women in the Scientific Search*. London: The Scarecrow Press.

Vare, Ethlie, Ann and Greg Ptacek, eds. (1993) *Women Inventors and Their Discoveries*. Minneapolis: Oliver Press.

Weber, Robert, L. (1988) *Pioneers of Science: Nobel Prize Winners in Physics*. Philadelphia: Hilger.

Wolpert, Lewis and Alison Richards. (1988) *A Passion for Science.* Oxford: Oxford University Press.

Yost, Edna. (1959) *Women of Modern Science.* New York: Dodd, Mead.

Zuckerman, Harriet. (1977) *Scientific Elite, Nobel Laureates in the United States.* New York: Macmillan.

1. Maria Mitchell

This chapter relied extensively on the following published sources:

Abir-Am and Dorina Outram. (1986) *Uneasy Careers and Intimate Lives: Women in Science, 1700-1945.* New Brunswick: Rutgers University Press.

Bennett, Wayne. (1973) *Women Who Dared to be Different.* Champaign, Il: Garrard Publishing Company.

Drake, Thomas, Edward. (1968) *A Scientific Outpost: The First Half century of the Nantucket Maria Mitchell Association.* Nantucket, MA: Nantucket Maria Mitchell Association.

Gormley, Beatrice. (1995) *Maria Mitchell; The Soul of an Astronomer.* Grand Rapids, MI: William B. Eerdmans Publishing Company.

Jones, Bessie Z. and Lyle G. Boyd. (1971) *The Harvard College Observatory: The First Four Directorships, 1839-1919.* Cambridge: Belknap Press of Harvard University Press.

Kass-Simon, G. and Patricia Farnes, eds. (1990) *Women in Science.* Bloomington: Indiana University Press.

Kendall, Phebe, Mitchell, ed. (1896) *Maria Mitchell: Life, Letters, and Journals.* Boston: Lee and Shepard Publications.

Kohlstedt, Sally, G. (1978) "Maria Mitchell: The Advancement of Women in Science." 15 *New England Quarterly.*

Oles, Carole. (1985) *Night Watches: Inventions on the Life of Maria Mitchell.* Cambridge, MA: Alice James Books.

Rossiter, Margaret, W. (1982) *Women Scientists in America: Struggles and Strategies to 1940.* Baltimore: The Johns Hopkins University Press.

Wright, Helen. (1950) *Sweeper in the Sky: The Life of Maria Mitchell, First Woman Astronomer in America.* New York: MacMillan Company.

2. Ellen H. Swallow Richards

This chapter relied extensively on the following published sources:

Clarke, Robert. (1973) *Ellen Swallow, The Woman Who Founded Ecology.* Chicago: Follett.

Douty, Esther Morris. (1961) *America's First Woman Chemist, Ellen Richards.* New York: Messner.

Hunt, Caroline, Louisa. (1958) *The Life of Ellen H. Richards, 1842-1911.* Washington: American Home Economics Association.

Kass-Simon, G. and Patricia Farnes, eds. (1990) *Women in Science.* Bloomington: Indiana University Press.

Pursell, Carroll, W., Jr., ed. (1990) *Technology in America: A History of Individuals and Ideas.* Cambridge, MA: MIT Press.

Richards, Robert, H. (1936) *Robert Hallowell Richards, His Mark.* Boston: Little, Brown & Company.

Rossiter, Margaret, W. (1982) *Women Scientists in America: Struggles and Strategies to 1940.* Baltimore: The Johns Hopkins University Press.

Vare, Ethlie, Ann. (1992) *Adventurous Spirit: A Story About Ellen Swallow Richards.* Minneapolis: Carolrhoda Books.

Yost, Edna. (1955) *American Women of Science*. Philadelphia: J.B. Lippincot Company.

3. *Marie Sklodowska Curie*

This chapter relied extensively on the following published sources:

Curie, Eve. (1937) *Madame Curie, a Biography*. New York: Doubleday.

Curie, Marie. (1923) *Pierre Curie*. New York: MacMillan.

Feuerlicht, Robert, Strauss. (1965) *Madame Curie; A Concise Biography*. New York: American R. D. M. Corporation.

Giroud, Francoise. (1986) *Marie Curie, a Life*. New York: Holmes & Meler.

Felder, Deborah, G. (1996) *The One Hundred Most Influential Women of All Time: A Ranking Past and Present*. Secaucus, N. J.: Carol Publishing Group.

Kass-Simon, G. and Patricia Farnes, eds. (1990) *Women in Science*. Bloomington: Indiana University Press.

McGrayne, Sharon, Bertsch. (1993) *Nobel Prize Women in Science*. New York: Birch Lane Press.

Pflaum, Rosalynd. (1989) *Grand Obsession: Madame Curie and Her World*. New York: Doubleday.

Pyclor, Helena, M., Nancy G. Slack, and Pnina G. Abir-Am, eds. (1996) *Creative Couples in Sciences*. New Brunswick, N.J.: Rutgers Univeristy Press.

Reid, Robert. (1974) *Marie Curie*. New York: E. P. Dutton.

Rossiter, Margaret, W. (1982) *Women Scientists in America: Struggles and Strategies to 1940*. Baltimore: The Johns Hopkins University Press.

Quinn, Susan. (1995) *Marie Curie: A Life.* New York: Simon & Schuster.

Weber, Robert, L. (1988) *Pioneers of Science: Nobel Prize Winners in Physics.* Philadelphia: Hilger.

4. Alice Hamilton

This chapter relied extensively on the following published sources:

Addams, Jane. (1910) *Twenty Years at Hull House.* New York: MacMillan Company.

Hamilton, Alice. (1943) *Exploring the Dangerous Trade: The Autobiography of Alice Hamilton, M.D.* Boston: Little, Brown.

Kass-Simon, G. and Patricia Farnes, eds. (1990) *Women in Science.* Bloomington: Indiana University Press.

Rossiter, Margaret, W. (1982) *Women Scientists in America: Struggles and Strategies to 1940.* Baltimore: The Johns Hopkins University Press.

Sicherman, Barbara. (1984) *Alice Hamilton, a Life in Letters.* Cambridge: Harvard University Press.

Slaight, W. R. (1974) *Alice Hamilton: First Lady of Industrial Medicine.* Ann Arbor: University Microfilms.

Yost, Edna. (1955) *American Women of Science.* Philadelphia: J.B. Lippincot Company.

5. Florence Rena Sabin

This chapter relied extensively on the following published sources:

Hume, R. F. (1964) *Great Women of Medicine.* New York: Random House.

Kass-Simon, G. and Patricia Farnes, eds. (1990) *Women in Science.* Bloomington: Indiana University Press.

Kaye, Judith. (1993) *The Life of Florence Sabin.* New York: Twenty-First Century Books.

Kronstadt, Janet. (1990) *Florence Sabin.* New York: Chelsea House.

Phelan, Mary, Kay. (1969) *Probing the Unknown: The Story of Dr. Florence Sabin.* New York: Thomas Y. Crowell Company.

Rossiter, Margaret, W. (1995) *Women Scientists in America; Before Affirmative Action 1940-1972.* Baltimore: Johns Hopkins University Press.

Rossiter, Margaret, W. (1982) *Women Scientists in America: Struggles and Strategies to 1940.* Baltimore: The Johns Hopkins University Press.

Yost, Edna. (1955) *American Women of Science.* Philadelphia: J.B. Lippincot Company.

6. Lillian Moller Gilbreth

This chapter relied extensively on the following published sources:

Gilbreth, Frank, B. and Lillian Moller Gilbreth. (1917) *Applied Motion Study; A Collection of Papers on the Efficient Method to Industrial Preparedness.* New York: Sturgis & Walton.

Gilbreth, Lillian. (1914) *The Psychology of Management: the Function of the Mind in Determining, Teaching, and Installing Methods of Least Waste.* New York: Sturgis and Walton.

Gilbreth, Lillian. (1951) *Living with our Children.* New York: Norton.

Kass-Simon, G. and Patricia Farnes, eds. (1990) *Women in Science.* Bloomington: Indiana University Press.

Rossiter, Margaret, W. (1995) *Women Scientists in America; Before Affirmative Action 1940-1972*. Baltimore: Johns Hopkins University Press.

Rossiter, Margaret, W. (1982) *Women Scientists in America: Struggles and Strategies to 1940*. Baltimore: The Johns Hopkins University Press.

Yost, Edna. (1955) *American Women of Science*. Philadelphia: J.B. Lippincot Company.

Yost, Edna. (1949) *Frank and Lillian Gilbreth, Partners for Life*. New Brunswick, N.J.: Rutgers University Press.

Gilbreth, Frank, Bunker and Ernestine Gilbreth Carey. (1948) *Cheaper by the Dozen*. New York: T. Y. Crowell Company.

7. Lise Meitner

This chapter relied extensively on the following published sources:

Alton, Jeannine. (1982) *Report on the Papers and Correspondence of Otto Robert Frisch*. London: Contemporary Scientific Archives Centre.

Crawford, Deborah. (1969) *Lise Meitner, Atomic Pioneer*. New York: Crown Publishers.

Frisch, Otto, Robert. (1979) *What Little I Remember*. New York: Cambridge University Press.

Frisch, Otto, Robert. (1978) "Lise Meitner, Nuclear Pioneer." *New Scientist* 9 November.

Frisch, Otto, Robert. (1965) *Working with Atoms*. New York: Basic Books.

Frisch, Otto, Robert. (1959) *Trends in Atomic Physics; Essays Dedicated to Lise Meitner, Otto Hahn, Max von Laue on the Occasion of their Eightieth Birthday*. New York: Interscience Publishers.

Hahn, Otto. (1970) *Otto Hahn: My Life.* New York: Herder.

Hermann, Armin. (1979) *The New Physics: The Route into the Atomic Age: In Memory of Albert Einstein, Max von Laue, Otto Hahn, Lise Meitner.* Bonn-Bad Godesberg: Inter Naitons.

Kass-Simon, G. and Patricia Farnes, eds. (1990) *Women in Science.* Bloomington: Indiana University Press.

McGrayne, Sharon, Bertsch. (1993) *Nobel Prize Women in Science.* New York: Birch Lane Press.

Perutz, M. F. (1997) "A Passion for Science." *The New York Review* 20 February.

Rossiter, Margaret, W. (1982) *Women Scientists in America: Struggles and Strategies to 1940.* Baltimore: The Johns Hopkins University Press.

Sime, Ruth, L. (1989) "Lise Meitner and the Discovery of Fission." 66 *Journal of Chemical Education.*

Sime, Ruth, L. (1996) *Lise Meitner: A Life in Physics.* Berkeley: University of California Press.

8. Emmy Noether

This chapter relied extensively on the following published sources:

Auguste, Dick. (1980) *Emmy Noether, 1882-1935.* Boston: Birkhauser.

Beyerchen, Alan, D. (1977) *Scientists Under Hitler: Politics and the Physics Community.* New Haven: Yale University Press.

Brewer, James, W. and Martha K. Smith, eds. (1981) *Emmy Noether: A Tribute to Her Life and Work.* New York: Marcel Dekker.

Dick, Auguste. (1981) *Emmy Noether, 1882-1935.* Boston: Birkhauser.

Kass-Simon, G. and Patricia Farnes, eds. (1990) *Women in Science.* Bloomington: Indiana University Press.

McGrayne, Sharon, Bertsch. (1993) *Nobel Prize Women in Science.* New York: Birch Lane Press.

Osen, Lynn, M. (1974) *Women in Mathematics.* Cambridge: MIT Press.

Rossiter, Margaret, W. (1982) *Women Scientists in America: Struggles and Strategies to 1940.* Baltimore: The Johns Hopkins University Press.

Srinivasan, Bhama and Judith Sally, eds. (1983) *Emmy Noether in Bryn Mawr: Proceedings of a Symposium.* New York: Springer-Verlag.

9. Leta Stetter Hollingworth

This chapter relied extensively on the following published sources:

Hollingworth, Harry, L. (1943) *Leta Stetter Hollingworth: A Biography.* Lincoln, Nebraska: University of Nebraska Press.

Hollingworth, Leta, S. (1927) *Gifted Children, their Nature and Nurture.* New York: The Macmillan Company.

Rossiter, Margaret, W. (1982) *Women Scientists in America: Struggles and Strategies to 1940.* Baltimore: The Johns Hopkins University Press.

Shields, Stephanie, A. (1975) Ms. Pilgrim's Progress: The Contributions of Leta Stetter Hollingworth to the Psychology of Women." 30 *American Psychologist.*

10. Gerty Theresa Radnitz Cori

This chapter relied extensively on the following published sources:

Cori, Carl. (1969) "The Call of Science." 38 *Annual Review of Biochemistry*.

Kass-Simon, G. and Patricia Farnes, eds. (1990) *Women in Science*. Bloomington: Indiana University Press.

McGrayne, Sharon, Bertsch. (1993) *Nobel Prize Women in Science*. New York: Birch Lane Press.

Ochao, Severo. (1958) "Gerty T. Cori: Biochemist." 126 *Science*.

Opfell, Olga. (1976) *The Lady Laureates*. Metuchen, New Jersey: Scarecrow Press.

Pycior, Helena, M., Nancy G. Slack, and Pnina G. Abir-Am, eds. (1996) *Creative Couples in Sciences*. New Brunswick, N.J.: Rutgers Univeristy Press.

Reynolds, Moira, Davison. (1997) *Immigrant American Women Role Models: Fifteen Inspiring Biographies, 1856-1950*. New York: United States McFarland & Company Inc.

Rossiter, Margaret, W. (1982) *Women Scientists in America: Struggles and Strategies to 1940*. Baltimore: The Johns Hopkins University Press.

11. Florence Seibert

This chapter relied extensively on the following published sources:

Rossiter, Margaret, W. (1995) *Women Scientists in America; Before Affirmative Action 1940-1972*. Baltimore: Johns Hopkins University Press.

Rossiter, Margaret, W. (1982) *Women Scientists in America: Struggles and Strategies to 1940.* Baltimore: The Johns Hopkins University Press.

Seibert, Florence, Barbara. (1968) *Pebbles on the Hill of a Scientist.* St. Petersburg.

Yost, Edna. (1955) *American Women of Science.* Philadelphia: J.B. Lippincot Company.

12. Barbara McClintock

This chapter relied extensively on the following published sources:

Dash, Joan. (1991) *Triumph of Discovery: Women Scientists Who Won the Nobel Prize.* Englewood Cliffs: Julian Messner.

Federoff, Nina, V. and David Botstein, eds. (1992) *The Dynamic Genomes: Barbara McClintock's Ideas in the Century of Genetics.* New York: Cold Spring Harbor Press.

Felder, Deborah, G. (1996) *The One Hundred Most Influential Women of All Time: A Ranking Past and Present.* Secaucus, N. J.: Carol Publishing Group.

Hacker, Carlotta. (1998) *Nobel Prize Winners.* New York: Crabtree Publishing.

Heiligman, Deborah. (1994) *Barbara McClintock: Alone in her Field.* New York: W. H. Freeman & Company.

Kass-Simon, G. and Patricia Farnes, eds. (1990) *Women in Science.* Bloomington: Indiana University Press.

Keller, Evelyn, Fox. (1983) *A Feeling for the Organism: The Life and Work of Barbara McClintock.* San Francisco: W. H. Freeman & Company.

Keller, Evelyn, Fox. (1981) "McClintock's Maize." 81 *Science.*

Kirkup, Gill and Laurie Smith Keller, eds. (1992) *Inventing Women: Science, Technology, and Gender.* Cambridge, MA: Polity Press in association with B. Blackwell and the Open University.

McClintock, Barbara. (1987) *The Discovery of Characterization of Transposable Elements: the Collected Papers of Barbara McClintock.* New York: Garland Park.

McGrayne, Sharon, Bertsch. (1993) *Nobel Prize Women in Science.* New York: Birch Lane Press.

Rossiter, Margaret, W. (1995) *Women Scientists in America; Before Affirmative Action 1940-1972.* Baltimore: Johns Hopkins University Press.

Rossiter, Margaret, W. (1982) *Women Scientists in America: Struggles and Strategies to 1940.* Baltimore: The Johns Hopkins University Press.

Shiels, Barbara. (1985) *Women and the Nobel Prize.* Minneapolis: Dillon Press.

Vare, Ethlie, Ann and Greg Ptacek, eds. (1993) *Women Inventors and Their Discoveries.* Minneapolis: Oliver Press.

13. *Maria Goeppert-Mayer*

This chapter relied extensively on the following published sources:

Dash, Joan. (1991) *Triumph of Discovery: Women Scientists Who Won the Nobel Prize.* Englewood Cliffs: Julian Messner.

Dash, Joan. (1973) *A Life of One's Own: Three Gifted Women and the Men they Married.* New York: Harper & Row.

Fermi, Laura. (1954) *Atoms in the Family*. Chicago: University of Chicago Press.

Gabor, Andrea. (1995) *Einstein's Wife: Work and Marriage in the Lives of Five Great Twentieth-century Women*. New York: Viking.

Goeppert-Mayer, Maria and J. Mayer. (1948) *Statistical Mechanics*. New York: Wiley & Sons.

Goeppert-Mayer, Maria. (1964) "The Shell Model." 92 *Science*.

Hall, Mary, Harrington. (1964) "The Nobel Genius." *San Diego Magazine* 5 August.

Hall, Mary, Harrington. (1964) "Maria Mayer: The Marie Curie of the Atom." 91 *McCalls*.

Johnson, Karen, E. (1986) "Maria Goeppert-Mayer: Atoms, Molecules and Nuclear Shells." 39 *Physics Today*.

Kass-Simon, G. and Patricia Farnes, eds. (1990) *Women in Science*. Bloomington: Indiana University Press.

McGrayne, Sharon, Bertsch. (1993) *Nobel Prize Women in Science*. New York: Birch Lane Press.

Rossiter, Margaret, W. (1995) *Women Scientists in America; Before Affirmative Action 1940-1972*. Baltimore: Johns Hopkins University Press.

Rossiter, Margaret, W. (1982) *Women Scientists in America: Struggles and Strategies to 1940*. Baltimore: The Johns Hopkins University Press.

Zuckerman, Harriet. (1977) *Scientific Elite; Nobel Laureates in the United States*. New York: MacMillan.

14. Rita Levi-Montalcini

This chapter relied extensively on the following published sources:

Dash, Joan. (1991) *Triumph of Discovery: Women Scientists Who Won the Nobel Prize.* Englewood Cliffs: Julian Messner.

Holloway, Marguerite. (1993) "Finding the Good in the Bad." *Scientific American* January.

Kass-Simon, G. and Patricia Farnes, eds. (1990) *Women in Science.* Bloomington: Indiana University Press.

Levi-Montalcini, Rita. (1988) *In Praise of Imperfection: My Life and Work.* New York: Basic Books.

Levi-Montalcini, Rita and Pietro Calissano. (1979) "The Nerve Growth Factor." 34 *Scientific American.*

McGrayne, Sharon, Bertsch. (1993) *Nobel Prize Women in Science.* New York: Birch Lane Press.

McGrayne, Sharon, Bertsch. (1996) "Nobel Prize Women in Science." AWIS May/June.

"Nobel Laureates Levi Montalcini, Cohen Share Prize for Pioneering Research Here." (1986) *Washington University in St. Louis Record* 11(10)/23 October.

15. Rosalind Franklin

This chapter relied extensively on the following published sources:

Berstein, Jeremy. (1978) *Experiencing Science.* New York: Basic Books.

Crick, Francis. (1988) *What Mad Pursuit: A Personal View of Scientific Discovery.* New York: Basic Books.

Judson, Horace, Freeland. (1986) "Annals of Science: The Legend of Rosalind Franklin." 6 *Science Digest.*

Judson, Horace, Freeland. (1979) *The Eighth Day of Creation.* New York: Simon and Schuster.

Kass-Simon, G. and Patricia Farnes, eds. (1990) *Women in Science.* Bloomington: Indiana University Press.

Klug, Aaron. (1968) "Rosalind Franklin and the Discovery of the Structure of DNA." 219 *Nature.*

McGrayne, Sharon, Bertsch. (1993) *Nobel Prize Women in Science.* New York: Birch Lane Press.

Olby, Robert. (1974) *Path to Double Helix.* Seattle: University of Washington Press.

Sayre, Anne. (1975) *Rosalind Franklin and DNA.* New York: W. W. Norton & Company.

Watson, James. (1968) *The Double Helix.* New York: Athenaeum.

16. Dorothy Mary Crowfoot Hodgkin

This chapter relied extensively on the following published sources:

Dodson, Guy, Jenny P. Glusker and David Sayre, eds. (1981) *Structural Studies on Molecules of Biological Interest; A Volume in Honor of Professor Dorothy Hodgkin.* Oxford: Clarendon Press.

Julian, Maureen, M. (1982) "Profiles in Chemistry: Dorothy Crowfoot Hodgkin, Nobel Laureate." 59 *Journal of Chemistry and Education.*

Kass-Simon, G. and Patricia Farnes, eds. (1990) *Women in Science.* Bloomington: Indiana University Press.

McGrayne, Sharon, Bertsch. (1993) *Nobel Prize Women in Science.* New York: Birch Lane Press.

Phillips, Patricia. (1990) *The Scientific Lady: A Social History of Women's Scientific Interests, 1520-1918*. London: Weidenfeld & Nicholson.

Wolpert, Lewis and Alison Richards. (1988) *A Passion for Science*. Oxford: Oxford University Press.

"The X-Ray Analysis of Complicated Molecules." (1965) 150 *Science*.